Outdoor Hobbies

Guy Williams

Outdoor Hobbies

Studio Vista

© 1967 Guy Williams

First published in Great Britain 1967 by
Studio Vista Limited, Blue Star House
Highgate Hill, London N19

Distributed in Canada by General Publishing Co. Ltd
30 Lesmill Road, Don Mills, Ontario

Set in 11pt Imprint

Printed in Great Britain by
The Garden City Press Limited
Letchworth, Hertfordshire

Contents

Introduction	7
Angling	9
Archaeology	18
Archery	28
Astronomy	33
Bird watching	38
Brass rubbing	42
Butterfly and moth hunting	46
Camping	51
Canoeing	60
Climbing and pot-holing	67
Collecting	70
Birds' eggs	70
Feathers	72
Pebbles	73
Pressed flowers	74
Seaweeds	76
Seeds	78
Shells	79
Signs	80
Skeleton leaves	81
Walking sticks	81
Cycling	83
Fossil hunting	89
Gardening	92
Gliding	99
Heraldry	100
Kite-making and kite-flying	107
Oil painting	113
Pets	121
Bantams	121
Cats	122
Dogs	123
Dormice	125
Goats	126
Guinea pigs	127
Hedgehogs	128
Pigeons and doves	129
Rabbits	130
Reptiles and amphibians	132
Photography	135
Ponds and pools	139
Pony trekking	143
Rambling	147
Running for pleasure	154
Rush basketry	156
Sightseeing	160
Sketching	169
Tracking	180
Water colour painting	184
Whittling	191

Introduction

How do you spend your time when you are out of doors? Are you fond of walking, or cycling?

These inexpensive ways of getting round the country are still popular. They bring us into close contact with nature and wild life, and with the sights and sounds and smells we associate with each particular season. Speedier, noisier and more up-to-date forms of transport seem to cut us off from these sources of pleasure.

Canoeing, too, has become something of a 'craze' recently as more and more young people have found out how enjoyable it is to journey in these very light craft along our incomparably beautiful rivers and canals. 'There is nothing—absolutely nothing,' you may remember Water Rat saying dreamily in Kenneth Grahame's immortal *The Wind in the Willows*, 'half so much worth doing as simply messing about in boats.'

Camping is now one of the most popular forms of holiday-making. What could be more exciting than waking up in the morning in comfort to hear birdsong, the music of running water, the stirrings of small animals, and all the scores of other sounds that can delight us if we remember to use our ears in the teeming countryside?

The great improvements made in camping equipment in recent years—the development of tents that are waterproof, roomy and portable, for instance, and improved facilities for cooking and sleeping—all make the need to 'rough it' in the countryside a thing of the past, except for spartan people who really enjoy cold hard ground, iron rations, and the harsh vagaries of our variable climate. Yes, the small hours can be extraordinarily chilly, even in the height of summer. So take a spare woollen garment or two if you leave for a camping expedition on a hot, sunny afternoon.

What if you live in a city or a large town, and mountains and moors and rivers seem depressingly far away?

You can still get out of doors and find plenty of interesting things to do in the parks and gardens that the guide books so rightly label our 'amenities'. This book has not been written only for people who can dash off to the seashore or the highlands at the drop of a hat. It is intended to appeal to everyone who has a sense of adventure and the will to enjoy life to the full, wherever he or she may be.

Angling

Angling is the most popular outdoor pastime bar none, and everyone who has at any time felt the thrill of having a fishing line tighten suddenly will know why. It is endlessly satisfying, because it is a hobby in which skill and judgement are more important than luck. It takes people to places of inexhaustible beauty and interest.

No wonder so many famous and heavily burdened men and women have sought pleasure and relaxation by salmon rivers or trout streams, or, if they have been really ambitious, in pursuit of tunny or barracuda or shark.

The fish you can catch. If you decide that angling is going to be *your* hobby (or one of your hobbies) you will want to know as soon as possible how much 'tackle' you will need, and what it is going to cost. The answers to these questions will depend to a great extent on the kind of fish you are going to try to catch, so we must first consider the different kinds of fish there are awaiting your attentions in fresh water. Sea fishing is a more complicated matter, and you should seek local information.

Salmon. This noble fish is migratory in its habits. Born in the smallest tributaries of sufficiently non-polluted rivers, it leaves when it is a few months old for its feeding grounds in the North Atlantic. Up to this stage, it is carefully protected, and if you do happen to hook one of the hungry 'parr' you should return it to the water. You can distinguish it from a trout quite easily by the regularly spaced finger-marks and the line of red spots on its flanks.

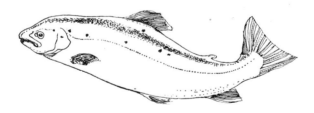

When the salmon returns from the sea, it may be caught with an artificial fly, a spinner or a worm, and it is sure to put up a thrilling fight. In the best rivers such as the Wye and the Dee fish that weigh 20 lb and more are not uncommon.

Seatrout or 'sewin'. Migratory trout that are, on average, a little smaller than salmon, but they fight just as fiercely. Best fished for at night, or in the very late evening.

Trout. A wonderfully sporting fish, that varies in size according to the food available in the water in which it lives. It may be caught in small mountain streams, lakes, ponds, reservoirs, and rivers as sluggish as the Thames. Small trout from fast-running waters are delicious when fried for breakfast in butter.

Grayling. Often caught in trouting waters, the grayling may be distinguished from its more highly prized neighbour by the impressive size of its dorsal fin.

If you are not lucky enough to be able to reach, or to be able to obtain permission to fish in waters that contain these four game members of the salmonidae family, you need not give up all thought of fishing. These widely distributed 'coarse' fish also give excellent sport:

Pike. Fierce and greedy, with a projecting underjaw and teeth as sharp as razors, pike may be caught in canals, as well as in rivers and lakes. Tempt them with artificial minnows, small fish, or spinning lures designed to look like these.

Chub. Useless for the pot, the chub nevertheless provides fine sport, growing in many cases to 5 or 6 lb before it encounters a hook.

Carp. An inhabitant of ponds and lakes, the carp may reach enormous sizes. Lurking in some gloomy depths there may be, now, a 50 lb monster waiting just for you—or for the bread, worms, maggots or potato you should take with you when you go looking for it.

Perch. Found both in pools and rivers, the perch is nearly as ungenerous in its nature as the pike. Large perch are very crafty and difficult to catch. Try worms, maggots, wasp grubs, or some similar small succulent creatures.

Roach. The roach, too, is found both in still and running water. It never seems to grow very large, but it is a prolific breeder and fills many keep-nets in the course of a year. Eats most of the known baits.

Rudd. Not unlike the roach, but with more pronounced colouring. The rudd is primarily a surface feeder, and may be taken with an artificial fly.

Tench. The tench, on the other hand, feeds almost exclusively near the bed of the pond or pool it inhabits. It is an attractive fish that provides excellent sport.

Other fish you may encounter in inland waters are *eel, barbel, bream, dace* and *gudgeon*. There are odd rarities, too, such as the *gwyniad* and the *char*, but it will be a red-letter day when you catch either of these.

Buying a rod. Give a lot of thought to the choice of your rod. The amount of pleasure you get from angling will depend largely on your getting a rod with the length, weight, balance and action that suits *you* best for the kind of fishing you are hoping to do.

Unfortunately, there is no such thing as an 'all-purpose' rod. A rod that is ideal for fly-fishing for trout may not have the right action at all for bait fishing, and vice versa. Until you have had quite a lot of experience it may be wise to seek the advice of an expert. If this is impossible, go to a reputable fishing tackle shop, explain your aims, and show a bias towards rods that are between 11 ft and 12 ft long, as this is a handy size. The rod you finally select should respond at once to the slightest movement of your wrist, while being well finished and strong enough to withstand all kinds of accidental rough treatment.

Your reel. Ideally, a reel should be chosen at the same time as the rod, as it will become almost an integral part of the butt once it is held in place by the rod's movable fixings.

There are several quite different types of reel from which to choose, but you will probably find that a Nottingham-type reel with a spring tension adjustment is most generally useful. Specially designed 'fixed-spool' reels can be obtained for spinning. These enable you to cast farther than the more usual revolving drum reel. They are great fun to use, but may be expensive, though they can be bought for as little as 25 shillings. Again, be prepared to seek expert advice in view of your local conditions.

A line. The modern nylon-type lines sold for anglers are so sound and so cheap that it is a good idea to have two or three lines of different thickness to suit various kinds of fishing. You will not enjoy fishing for (say) small mountain trout with the strong tackle needed to bring a specimen pike or carp to the bank. But remember that with skill a line of 2 or 3 lb breaking strain can bring in large fish. Four or five pounds would be a good strength to start with.

Casts. Artificial gut that is both inexpensive and reliable, can now be bought by the reel. You will need more than one thickness so that you can make up suitable casts:

A cast that is too thick will discourage more fish than a thin cast. A cast that is too thin will be liable to break, so that you lose your fly or hook—and, perhaps, a worthy fish as well.

To get good sport without wasting tackle it is essential to strike the right balance between these two extremes. Make sure that your cast

11

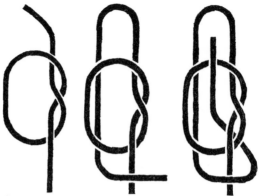

Taverner's Loop—useful for making a loop at the end of a cast

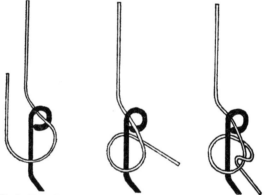

The Half Hitch Jam by which a hook may be quickly, neatly and easily attached to a cast

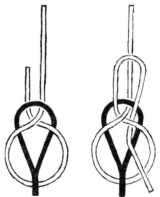

This shows how a cast and line may be joined

is slightly weaker than your line, otherwise, if you hit a snag, you may lose all your tackle.

Flies. It would be difficult to find a more exacting and exciting hobby than fishing for trout, seatrout or salmon with an artificial fly. If you would like to try it, don't be rushed into buying an extensive and expensive collection of flies—many veteran anglers fish most successfully with three or four trusted favourites. These notes may help you to choose wisely:

Artificial flies may be roughly divided into two categories—'wet' flies and 'dry' flies. Wet flies are fished in a submerged state, and usually represent spent flies or the nymphs of flies that have grown up from the egg stage in water. Dry flies are intended to remain on the surface of the water, and usually represent 'duns'—flies that have just emerged from their underwater skins, and are resting momentarily before they fly off inland—or 'spinners', which are the egg-layers.

A 'hatch' of one particular type of fly may attract the hungry attentions of all the trout in the vicinity. Therefore, it will pay you to observe as carefully as possible the natural food that the fish are at any given moment actually taking. Some flies, such as the Mayfly, may only be effective during certain short flurries of fishy excitement. Other good old standbys such as the March Brown may be killers in all but the close season.

Salmon and seatrout flies are invariably larger than trout flies, and usually more exotic. They are tied on stronger hooks, too, for obvious reasons.

Casting. Before you go fly-fishing, you may like to practise casting, for it is not very easy to put a fly exactly where you want it on the water without undue effort and without an alarming splash.

A large lawn is a good place for practising. Don't put a cast or a hook on the end of your line, just concentrate on moving your right wrist and forearm so that your rod tip moves backwards in a smooth arc, drawing your line out into a straight line behind you. Wait until the line is right out behind you. Then it should travel forwards again, so that the line is thrown out in front of you until it stops a little above, and parallel to, the ground. If you keep the rod quite still at that stage, the line should fall gently, in a straight line, to the ground (later, of course, it should fall to the water in the same controlled and unobtrusive way). To see where the line is falling you may like to tie a brightly coloured feather on the end.

Successful casting is largely a matter of timing. As you gain experience, you will be able to judge to a nicety the length of the pause necessary between the end of the upward movement of your wrist and the start of the downward and forward movement. If you cut this pause too short, your line may crack like a whip.

How to fish with a fly. Having practised casting, and having access to some suitable water, you will want to try your luck. Get into the habit of studying from some suitable cover each pool or race before you get too close to it. Your aim should be to know where the fish are likely to be lying so that you can decide how best to approach them.

In all normal circumstances, fish feeding in running water will be poised with their mouths turned into the current, so you will stand a better chance of offering them a meal without alarming them if you work your way upstream. Some fish are extremely shy, and even the glint of a shiny rod may put them down.

There are several different ways in which water can be 'covered', or fished thoroughly—you may even find it necessary to cast downstream occasionally if trees or other obstructions make upstream casting impracticable.

When you are trying to hook one particular fish—one that you have seen rising, perhaps—try to drop your fly lightly on the surface of the water a few feet upstream and then draw it gently over your quarry by raising the tip of your rod.

It is a great thrill when a fish takes your fly, but you must be ready to 'strike', to drive home the barbed end of the hook, by a quick movement of your wrist or you may have attracted that fish in vain. Never allow your line to go unnecessarily slack or you will miss the vital messages from the end of it on which your prompt action will depend.

Coarse fishing. In many waters, and for certain kinds of fish, the use of artificial flies is impracticable, or unlikely to bring success. Then, a bait of some kind may be offered on a carefully chosen hook. Here are some of the possible alternatives:

Worms. You will be able to find plenty of suitable worms by digging in your garden, or by going out at night with a torch. Redworms and brandlings can be found under stones, or in piles of rotting vegetation.

All worms should be 'scoured' before they are used as bait, as this makes them tougher, and, it seems, more appetizing to the fish. To scour, put some fresh moss and a little fine sand in a properly ventilated container from which the worms cannot escape, and leave them there for a few days, turning the container over occasionally to keep the worms moving. If worms are to be kept for a week or more before they are used they should be fed with grass, cabbage leaf or bread that has been dipped in milk.

Maggots or 'gentles'. These are the grubs of the bluebottle or blowfly. They can be bought from dealers all the year round, or bred at home (if you have a strong enough stomach) during the summer months.

To start a maggot farm, you will need a box in which you can

14

fix a 'false floor' made of fine mesh wire netting. This should be an inch or two above the real floor, which should be covered with clean sand. On the netting, place a few slices of raw meat or liver, and leave the lid of the box ajar (or make some holes in the side) so that the flies can enter to lay their eggs. When the maggots are large enough to be of interest to fish they will fall through the netting on to the sand.

Bread. This, the most easily obtained of all baits, is appreciated by the majority of the coarse fish you are likely to encounter. You can cut cubes or the crust from a loaf just as it comes from the baker, you can use pieces of toast, or you can make paste by kneading wet bread into lumps.

Using a float. A float is used to control the depth to which a baited hook will sink in the water. You can make a float quite easily from a swan or goose quill, or even, in an emergency, from a reed or a piece of stick, but commercially made floats are not expensive.

At first, you may find it rather difficult to judge just where on your cast the float should be fixed. Ideally, you should know how deep the water is (you can use a small weight on the end of a thin plumbline if you are sure that you are not going to disturb the fish you are aiming to catch).

Then, if you want your bait to be offered to the fish six inches (say) above the bottom of the swim, you can easily subtract this from the average depth and so find the correct position for the float.

You can buy some split lead shot to fasten on your cast, too, so that the float is sensitively balanced. Then the slightest alteration in the tension of the cast will make the visible portion of the float tilt and turn and warn you that you may have attracted something!

Two other very common methods of fishing are spinning and ledgering. In spinning a bright object is drawn through the water to attract the fish. In ledgering the bait is kept on the bottom in one place by a heavy weight and allowed to stay there for a long time. Neither method uses a float.

Ground bait. Experienced anglers will often persuade the fish in a swim to feed by plying them with ground bait. Bread, bran, crushed maize and various meals can be used, the aim being to stimulate the fishes' appetites without satisfying them, and to attract other fish to the area. If you decide to use ground bait, throw your handfuls a little way upstream—how far will depend on the current, the depth of the water, and the weight of the bait.

Landing a fish. The minutes that follow the hooking of a fish are usually very exciting, especially if the fish on the end of the line is a big one, or an energetic fighter.

Your first concern when playing a fish will be to bring your catch as quickly and safely as possible to the bank, or to shallow water close by you where you can deal with it competently. Inevitably, a game fish will try to take the line towards any submerged rocks, roots or branches that will give it a chance to foul or break the cast. Your job will be to keep the fish away from such hazards by bending your rod back and by applying sideward pressure until eventually the fish tires, and can be brought within reach of your hands.

A landing net is almost essential for all but the very smallest fish, but even a wide strong net will not guarantee a successful capture unless you use it with skill and discretion—it is remarkable how an apparently exhausted fish will revive and make off like an electric flash once it catches sight of the mesh! To prevent this, put the net down into the water and get it quite motionless before you guide the fish towards it. Then, as you steer the fish over the frame of the net, raise the net as deftly and smoothly as you can. Any sudden or unnecessary movements at this critical juncture may well cost you your fish.

Other items of equipment. You may like to consider these additional items of equipment that will allow you to fish farther afield, and in greater comfort.

A fishing basket, box or bag. You will have quite a lot to carry by the time you have collected all your tackle, so a hold-all of some kind is virtually essential. A stiff-sided container is preferable to a floppy bag, as some items of your equipment—your reels, for instance—will be liable to get damaged on difficult journeys unless they are protected.

Smaller containers. You will find some smaller boxes, tins and cartons useful for holding hooks, floats, lead weights, and other easily lost essentials. One of these containers should hold a pair of scissors, a penknife, a pin, small pliers for the shot, and any other implements you think you may need.

A keep net. Normally, you will probably be content to return to the water, alive, all the fish you catch that you do not need for the table—even 'specimen' fish can be an embarrassment once they have been on dry land so long that the delight and surprise have worn off. If you are going in for competitive angling, you will need a 'keep net' in which your captives can swim until they are officially weighed. It is a good idea to include in your equipment some scales in which to weigh your fish.

A tape measure or foot rule may be useful for recording the dimensions of the fish you land.

A rod rest. When you are coarse fishing, you may not want to stand with your rod in your hand during the whole of a day's sport. It is easy to make a rod rest by trimming a forked twig so that you can drive the shank into the ground.

Waders. For some types of fishing—for salmon-fishing in wide rivers, for instance—waders or thigh boots are almost essential. Even in more sedate waters, a pair of Wellingtons may enable you to reach good lies that you would otherwise have to leave unfished. Macintoshes and waterproof capes may be a bit of a burden, but they may make fishing practicable even on a very wet day. It is worthwhile remembering that you can often feel unpleasantly cold and damp by the water's edge when nothing exciting is happening to distract you from your physical condition. Once you hook a fish, of course, all your discomforts will be forgotten.

Further reading
MICHAEL SHEPHARD, *Instructions to Young Anglers* (Museum Press).
TAG BARNES, *Coarse Fishing for Absolute Beginners* (Studio Vista).
HARVEY CORBETT, *Coarse Fishing* (Museum Press).

2—OH

Archaeology

In the nineteenth century, archaeology was a hobby that appealed mainly to elderly, wealthy and slightly inefficient amateurs. Many of these people spent their spare time spoiling irreplaceable sites in their frantic rush to find hidden antiquities. Nowadays, archaeology is an exact science, in which skilful experts study men of the past, not only by reading their writings, but by excavating their homes, their sacred monuments and even their graves. Although we cannot hope to find out the thoughts of our remote ancestors by our researches, we can get a very good picture of how they lived, and we can realize to an exciting extent how they managed to deal with the problems of their time.

How to begin. Unfortunately, you cannot become a successful archaeologist just by going out and digging blindly wherever you think there may be remains of the distant past hidden beneath the surface of the soil. Like all hobbies that have a scientific bias, archaeology can only be enjoyed to the full by people who are prepared to do a little study.

There are several ways in which you can acquire the necessary knowledge. Here are a few suggestions:

Books. Most bookshops and public libraries contain a number of books on archaeology written by experts. You will also be able to get a lot of interesting data from the journals published by various archaeological societies. These usually contain reports of actual digs that you will find instructive. Your librarian will probably be able to give you up-to-the-minute information about them.

Societies. Most districts contain a number of people who are interested in the history of the locality. Often these people will belong to an archaeological society or some similar body. By joining them, you will be able to find out if any sites are due to be excavated within easy reach of your home, and if you are lucky you will be able to volunteer to help at one of these.

Lectures. These are given periodically at most museums, and courses are arranged by the Workers' Educational Association (WEA) (Headquarters, 27 Portman Square, London, W1), by the extra-mural departments of most universities, and by many local education authorities. Lecture courses are often run in conjunction with practical work, and so they may be a useful 'lead in' to research in the field.

Additional informative publications are listed on page 27.

Observation. Even if you are unable at first to take part in any practical archaeological research under expert guidance, you will be able to get a lot more pleasure from the time you spend out of doors if you keep your eyes open, and if you look for evidence of early settlements. Many famous archaeological sites have been discovered by people who were quick to notice unusual features in farming territory or undisturbed landscape, and it may happen that you have some fascinating antiquity right on your doorstep, though nobody guesses it is there.

To distinguish between natural and man-made features, it will help you to have a large scale map that shows how prehistoric sites are distributed in the district you are studying. Most earthworks, such as defensive banks and ditches, trackways, the footings of ancient buildings and burial mounds or barrows, are clearly marked on one inch to the mile Ordnance Survey maps. Make a point of seeking these out. Examine them closely from as many different angles as possible, and you will soon learn to recognize the contours and changes of plane that betray the presence of an archaeological feature.

When you are looking for sites that have not been discovered previously and charted, you will probably find that the early morning and the late evening offer the best opportunities. At those times, when the sun's rays strike the earth obliquely, the shadows that result accentuate changes of plane that would not be visible at all under midday conditions.

Celtic fields. When you are out walking or cycling in the countryside you may look for the small square or nearly square plots of ground that were cultivated in Bronze Age, Iron Age and Roman times. They are now merged so completely into the landscape that they are almost invisible, but occasionally, when lighting conditions are favourable, you will be able to see the small steps and terraced surfaces formed by the gradual downhill movement of the loosened soil. Archaeologists call these barely perceptible steps 'lynchets', the step on the uphill side of a field being known as a 'positive' lynchet and that on the downhill side being known as a 'negative' lynchet.

Crop marks. You may look for 'crop marks', too. These are variations in the surface of massed vegetation that indicate the existence of archaeological features in the soil beneath.

Let us take, as an example, the foundations of a prehistoric hut. Where masonry is buried, the plants above it may not be able to develop long roots or obtain water for growth when the weather is very dry. So, in times of drought, you may be able to trace the layout of a vanished building by noticing where the vegetation is shorter or sparser than that on the surrounding surfaces, and where it has a tendency to wither away.

Where deep holes have been dug, to support upright posts and other structural members, or to act as storage pits for grain, or as rubbish dumps, the soil is often deep and rich. There, more water

19

will be retained, the roots of the plants will be able to penetrate to lower levels, and the vegetation will be taller and stronger than that on the surrounding surfaces.

The Old Stone Age. Leaving for later consideration the treasures you may uncover on an actual 'dig', let us look next at some more of the discoveries you can make as you wander round the countryside, relating each to some specific period, so that you will get the additional excitement of knowing how old (to within a few hundred, or a few thousand, years) the evidence you are observing may be.

The most remote period that is likely to concern you is the Old Stone Age, when man was in a primitive state of physical development and technical attainment. The Old Stone Age went on for so long that during it no fewer than four major ice advances occurred in the Northern Hemisphere, or so it is believed. The earliest of these is generally referred to as the 'Gunz glaciation', and it occurred approximately 570,000 years ago. The most recent is the Wurm glaciation, which occurred about 70,000 years ago.

Undoubtedly, the only identifiable artefacts (or man-made tools) you are likely to find after so long a lapse of time are the hard, imperishable flint implements that were shaped by palaeolithic craftsmen with so much skill. In the British Museum and in the Natural History Museum at South Kensington you can see collections of cutters, scrapers and axes that trace the whole known development of the flint-shaper's technique.

There is no point in looking for flint tools and implements in places to which they cannot possibly have been carried. Before you start searching, think of the kind of places a primitive huntsman would frequent—river banks are particularly worthwhile, for there animals

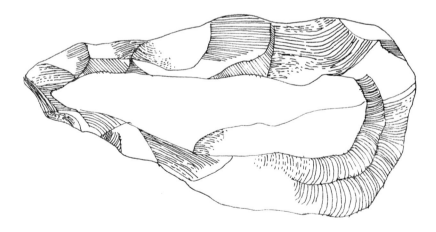

Paleolithic hand axe

20

could be waylaid when they came down to the water's edge to drink. After they had been killed, they would be skinned and, probably, dismembered. Inevitably, a number of flint spear tips and knives would be lost or discarded during the hunt and subsequent processes.

The Mesolithic Period. After the last Ice Advance the climate of Europe gradually improved, and deciduous vegetation spread northwards until most of the lower ground forms were shrouded in a dense and continuous wood or thicket. The period of time between about 14,000 BC and 4000 BC is usually known as the Mesolithic Period, and from the amateur archaeologist's point of view it is particularly well worth studying, because mesolithic flint tools and weapons are small, beautifully worked, and reasonably easy to find. As a rule, a mesolithic knife, arrow or harpoon would be made by setting one or more tiny razor-sharp blades called 'microliths' in a bone or wooden shaft. You can make a most interesting collection of these microliths if you keep your eyes open when you are pottering about on beaches, sand dunes, upland moors, sandy heaths and other places where the vegetation, in mesolithic times, would probably have been sparse enough to favour encampment.

The Neolithic and Bronze Age. About 2700 BC a notable wave of migrants came to Britain from Europe. Being farmers, rather than hunters, they chose to settle on the light-soiled and easily worked

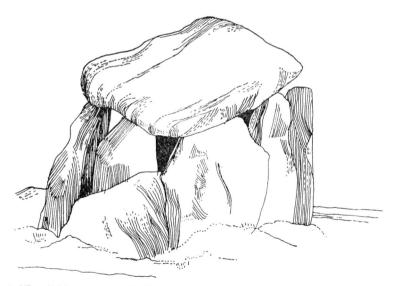

A Megalithic tomb, originally covered by stones and turf

chalklands in the south. Unfortunately, nearly all traces of their dwellings have disappeared owing to the rapid erosion of the land on which they lived, but there are still plenty of neolithic burial mounds and barrows you can study. You may also like to visit and examine one of the strange circular earthworks that archaeologists call 'causewayed camps'. Several of these are to be seen in the chalk country of southern Britain. They may have been used as cattle enclosures.

Megaliths. Among the most impressive survivals from the Neolithic Period are the communal tombs built with large slabs of stone, dry stone walling, and great quantities of earth. These are usually known as 'megaliths', and there are several examples in and near the Cotswolds. In some cases the earth covering has been washed away during the intervening centuries and only the stone components are left. Don't pay too much attention to any local inhabitants who may try to assure you that 'them stones were put there by the Druids'. They weren't! The Druids were priests who operated much later, during the Iron Age.

Stonehenge. About 1600 BC, there seems to have developed in Britain a body of very enterprising traders who acquired great wealth by passing gold from the Wicklow Mountains of Ireland to the thriving communities in Central Europe and by the Eastern Mediterranean. This social development is generally known as the 'Wessex Culture', and finds from Wessex-type barrows provide some of the most unusual and magnificent treasures in the archaeological sections of the great museums.

The world famous site of Stonehenge started its existence in late neolithic times. Originally, it consisted of a circular bank and ditch, which enclosed a ring of cremation pits. It was only one of several similar monuments, or 'henges', each of which was approached by a processional way leading from a river. The position of the sun or the stars at some significant date is believed to have controlled the general layout of a henge.

In the days of the Wessex chiefs, Stonehenge was considerably 'improved', a horseshoe-shaped part-circle of great sarsen stones being added, with a stone lintel across each pair of sarsens, a circle of upright bluestones, and a circle of upright sarsens with a continuous lintel. The bluestones are particularly interesting because they must have been brought, partly by water, from the Prescelly Mountains in South Wales.

Iron Age hill forts. The Iron Age was a period of considerable unrest in Europe, as the Celtic tribes on the Continent were spreading outwards and seeking new lands on which to settle. By the middle of the third century BC the influx of La Tène tribes had become a serious menace to those who had already settled in Britain, so, to repel the intruders, elaborate hill forts were constructed, many of which we can still see if we look up at the skyline today.

A visit to a large Iron Age hilltop fort can be a most exciting experience. For one thing, the elevated site will almost certainly ensure a magnificent view of the surrounding countryside. Most of the forts are splendidly constructed, too, with defensive banks and ditches built and dug at consistent heights, so that they appear to encircle the high ground like contour lines.

Roman Britain. 'The glory that was Greece, And the grandeur that was Rome' . . . You probably know that quotation of Edgar Allan Poe, and you may already be aware of the pervasive power of the Roman civilization, reminders of which can still be studied all over Western Europe.

As a start, you may like to study the system of roads designed by the Romans to ensure that their legions could cross the country as quickly as possible, without any fear of being ambushed while they were on the march.

It is sometimes said that Roman roads were absolutely straight, but this is not altogether correct. Usually, they were laid out in straight sections that ran between sighting points along the route. At regular intervals, there were forts and marching camps at which the troops could rest and take refreshment. Evidence of these defensive points is still being discovered today.

On the Ordnance Survey maps of southern Britain you will see many sites marked 'Roman Villa'. The word 'villa' does not mean a comfortable place at which the members of a wealthy family could reside in luxury and idleness—a villa was definitely a working place, with a farmyard, stables, workshops and barns. Even so, the living rooms would usually be pleasantly equipped and decorated, and the mosaic floors that survive (as, for example, at the villas at Chedworth

The Bath Gorgon

23

in Gloucestershire and at Lullingstone in Kent) are really impressive.

To amuse the inhabitants of the larger towns and the soldiers in the main garrisons, amphitheatres were built, so that shows of various kinds could be given—some of these were remarkably cruel. You can inspect reasonably well preserved amphitheatres at St Albans in Hertfordshire ('Verulamium') and at Chester ('Deva'). Traces of an amphitheatre in a bleak, isolated spot can be seen at Tomen-y-Mur, near Bala, in North Wales.

The post-Roman periods. After the Romans withdrew their forces from Britain there was a period two or three centuries long during which building and road-making virtually ceased. The inhabitants of Britain at that time, however, have left us a wealth of other memorials. Their pagan cemeteries have yielded great quantities of jewellery, dress accessories such as pins and brooches, weapons, table utensils, drinking horns, and work boxes of various kinds. Many of these have been discovered by accident, when older sites were being excavated or when fields were being ploughed. The treasures found in 1939 at Sutton Hoo near Woodbridge in Suffolk are among the most magnificent exhibits in the British Museum.

After the sixth century AD, the spread of Christianity increased the need for more permanent buildings, and you may enjoy looking out for the few surviving late Saxon churches (the three at Bradford-on-Avon in Wiltshire, at Deerhurst in Gloucestershire and at Earls Barton in Northamptonshire are particularly noteworthy) and for the more numerous buildings in which a few Saxon details can be identified. Norman churches and abbeys can still be seen in an excellent state of preservation, and buildings that date from more recent periods often contain features of interest to the antiquarian. You can read about some of these in the section of this book that deals with sightseeing.

Going on a dig. The idea of opening a site, or a suspected site, and of digging down through it with a spade, finding Sutton Hoo-type treasures on the way is a delightful one that appeals to the romantic side of nearly every one of us. Unfortunately, archaeological excavations just aren't like that. They are intended to give as complete a picture as possible of the various archaeological layers of the soil, and of their relationships with each other. This is a job that can only be properly carried out by trained experts who have studied the great sequence of changing styles and decorations used for ordinary objects. But even an expert will need assistance—and that is how you can start!

Let us assume, then, that you have volunteered to help with a dig, and that you have been interviewed and accepted by the director.

The first thing you will want to know is where you are going to stay. If the dig is near your home, or near suitable lodgings, this will present no unusual problems. Sometimes, though, it may be necessary for the diggers to camp near their site. When this happens, see that your equipment is entirely adequate and even above ordinary camping standards. Digging often begins at 9 a.m., and it may be 6 p.m. before work stops for the day. You will have had quite enough physical exercise by that time, and the idea of returning to a sparse heap of damp and uncomfortable bedding will not seem very attractive. (See *Camping*, p. 51.)

See, too, that you are properly equipped for the work in hand.

There are certain tools and implements that will normally be provided by the director of the dig. These are the heavier and more cumbersome items such as spades, picks, forks and wheelbarrows. The surveying equipment, too, will be his responsibility. The lighter items you will be expected to provide, and you will not enjoy the dig to the full unless you have chosen them with care. Here are some suggestions:

A trowel. Get a pointing trowel, preferably a 5 in. one which has the blade and the tang cast in one piece. Riveted trowels are rarely strong enough.

A hand brush. For removing loose soil. The stiff nylon carpet brushes sold for household use are excellent for archaeology. Smaller brushes, such as 1 in. and ½ in. housepainting brushes and the sable brushes used for watercolour painting may also be useful in special circumstances.

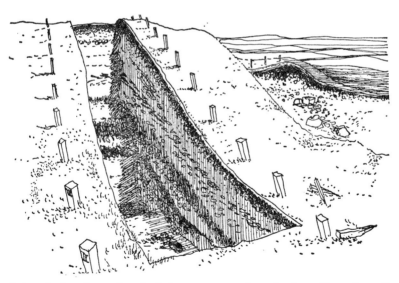

A trench dug for archaeological purposes explores in three dimensions. It opens up in two dimensions the area of an ancient site, and the archaeologist digs downward through layers representing earlier and earlier periods of time. The pairs of pegs on each side of the trench are used for taking measurements

25

An entrenching tool. Various implements can be bought from army surplus stores that are excellent for lifting turf, as well as being useful as small, easily manipulated picks.

A plasterer's leaf. This is an ideal implement for probing and scraping when light careful handling is essential. A steel knitting needle may also prove useful.

All your tools should be plainly marked with your initials, wherever this is possible. Metal tools may have a painted mark, or some other point of identification. It is annoying to have to waste time sorting out equipment and returning it to the rightful owners at the end of a long day's work if nothing has been done in advance to make this operation easier.

The choice of clothing is largely a matter of comfort and convenience. Heavy boots and shoes are not really suitable, because they can cause damage to fragile objects still hidden in a trench. Light rubber-soled shoes are usually recommended.

Normally, you will be fully instructed in what you are to do by the director of the dig, or by some experienced person he deputes to do this for him. You will be shown how to set out reference pegs, and how to take measurements from them. You will be taught how to 'take down' a layer, recording meticulously every object you find, even the little things that may seem unimportant at the time. You

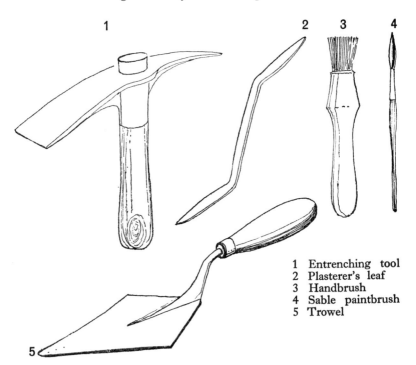

1 Entrenching tool
2 Plasterer's leaf
3 Handbrush
4 Sable paintbrush
5 Trowel

will be kept busy washing fragments of pottery and putting them into brown paper bags and labelling them with the details of the site, trench, layer, date, and the digger responsible. By the time you have done three days' digging, under careful supervision, you will feel like a knowledgeable expert yourself!

Further reading
A. V. B. GIBSON, *Instructions in Archaeology* (Museum Press).
STUART PIGGOTT, *Approach to Archaeology* (Adam & Charles Black).
STANLEY THOMAS, *Pre-Roman Britain* (Studio Vista).

Periodicals
The Calendar of Excavations. Published by the Council for British Archaeology, 10 Bolton Gardens, London, SW5 (Monthly, during the summer).
The Archaeological Newsletter. Obtainable from the Archaeological Newsletter, 60 Frederick Street, Gray's Inn Road, London, WC1. Published about once a month, it contains details of many current and future excavations, including those likely to be of interest to the beginner.

Archery

Archery developed as a matter of life and death. Only his skill with a bow and arrows would stand between many a primitive cave man and starvation; the crucial part played by bowmen at Crecy, Poitiers, Agincourt, and other vital battles of the Middle Ages is graphically recorded; even as recently as the nineteenth century the accurate marksmanship of the North American Indian was a deciding factor in many frontier skirmishes. Nowadays, archery is a pleasant and comparatively leisurely hobby, but it retains an unique interest for us, on account of its ancient history.

Some very authoritative books have been written about contemporary archery (you will find the names of a few at the end of this section) but there is no better way of finding out about the possibilities and limitations of this carefully organized pastime than by joining an archery club or association, if one exists in your district. Write to:

The Grand National Archery Society (Secretary: John J. Bray, 20 Broomfield Road, Chelmsford, Essex) for up-to-date information.

Buying a bow. There are only three items of equipment to be found before you can try archery for the first time—a bow, a bow-string and an arrow. Let's consider them in that order.

The traditional 'long bow' used by the heroes of English history was nearly always a 'self bow'—that is, made from one kind of wood, which was usually yew. It was at least five feet long, and sometimes as much as eighteen or nineteen inches longer than that. Nowadays, suitably aged yew wood is in short supply, and bows are often made from other woods such as osage and lemonwood, or even from metal or fibreglass. The use of these up-to-date materials seems in no way to decrease a bow's potential efficiency.

Don't be taken in by some phrase such as 'forty pounds' used in the description of a bow. This does not mean the physical weight of the bow, but the foot-pounds of energy needed to bring the bow to its full draw. It is important to choose a bow that is well within your available strength. So much depends on this that it is difficult to recommend specific weights for any age group. The following table may serve, however, as general guidance.

Juniors 18 lb – 28 lb (28 lb for a boy of 16)
Ladies 28 lb (average) (23 lb for a girl of 16)
Experienced archers 36 lb

Arrows. It is important, too, to buy or make your arrows in matched sets—usually, in threes, or in multiples of three. You will never be able to achieve consistent marksmanship with arrows of unequal length, weight, or resilience or 'spine'.

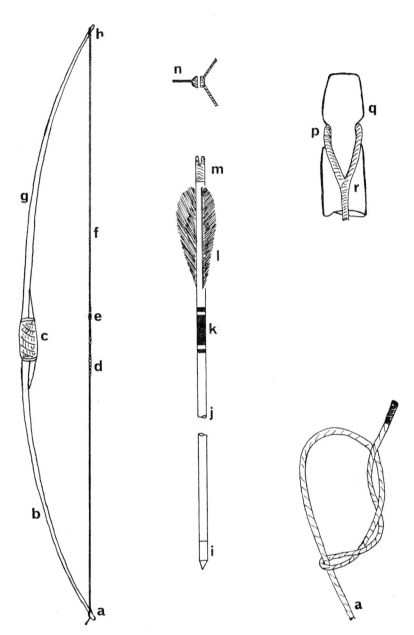

a timber hitch; b lower limb; c grip; d centre serving; e nocking point; f bow string; g upper limb; h nock; i pile; j shaft; k cresting; l fletching; m nock; n cock feather; p loop on upper nock; q bow nock; r belly of bow

Get some reasonably cheap arrows for your first attempts at archery, for your wastage rate may possibly be high. As soon as you can aim with confidence, invest in some really well-made arrows, for accuracy is impossible with indifferently fletched (or feathered) shafts.

Test an arrow for length by placing the slotted end (or 'nock') against your chest. Then if you extend your arms forward with the arrow between them the tips of your fingers should reach exactly as far as the 'pile' or tip of the arrow.

Bowstrings. Bowstrings are normally made from linen thread, or from the synthetic fibres Terylene or Fortisan. They are usually reinforced or whipped at the ends and in the centre to minimize wear.

There are two kinds to choose from—strings with one loop, and strings with two. The former have to be tied with a hitch to the lower nock on the bow, the loop being then slipped over the upper nock. Double loop strings, being of a definite and unalterable length, have to be made or chosen to suit a particular bow, at a particular draw weight, exactly.

When a bowstring fits a bow exactly, the 'fistmele' (or distance between the belly of the bow and the bowstring) should be between six and seven inches. If the bow is not sufficiently braced, accurate archery will be impossible. If it is overbraced, there is a distinct chance that the bow may snap.

Protective clothing. After you have shot a few trial arrows, you may find that the pads of your 'string fingers' are becoming sore. To protect them, you can wear an ordinary leather glove, or, better still, you can buy a skeleton glove or 'tab', or you can make one from a suitable piece of supple leather.

You may find that a 'bracer' is essential for comfortable shooting, too. This is a stiff leather shield which will protect the inside of your left arm from painful contact with the descending bowstring.

Shooting. The procedure that has to be gone through before an arrow flies on its way towards a target is carefully laid down and has been followed by successful archers for at least five centuries. There are five distinct phases:

The Stance. You will shoot most successfully if you are standing comfortably, with your shoulder line exactly at right angles to the front surface of the target. Put your feet a little way apart—how far, is a matter of personal preference—and then turn your head to the left (if you are right handed) so that you are looking at the target from over your left shoulder.

Nocking the arrow. Your bowstring should fit comfortably in the nock or slot at the end of each of your arrows without being so cramped that it is difficult to disengage. By the time you are ready

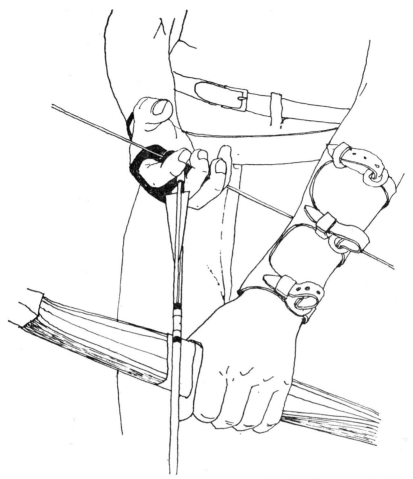

The 'Mediterranean Lock'

to draw, the arrow should be at right angles to the bow, on the left side of the centre, and touching it exactly midway between the ends of the bowstring.

Drawing the bow. It is not necessary, or even advisable, to grip the nock end of the arrow tightly when you are drawing the bow. The most useful hold to learn is the 'Mediterranean lock', in which the forefinger, middle finger and ring finger co-operate in taking the weight of the string, the nock end of the arrow being located between the forefinger and the middle finger. When the bow is fully drawn, the base of the tip or pile of the arrow will be level with the back or target side of the bow.

The hold. This is the momentary pause you will make while you check your stance and your aim. You will remember, of course, that an arrow flies in a parabolic curve, not in a straight line. Therefore, you may not need to aim directly at the centre of the target but at a point directly above it (if you are shooting from a distant mark) or at a point a little below it (if you are shooting from a shorter distance). Then comes

The release. This often seems the hardest part of the whole procedure to carry out successfully. The string is pulled hard into the chin by the hook of the last joint of the three fingers, care being taken not to bend the base knuckles of the fingers, but to keep them flat, and to grip the string, not the arrow, with these three fingers. The release is accomplished by pulling the fingers off the string as it is held against the chin. The top surface of the first finger slides back under the jaw, and keeps contact with it as the fingers open. Make sure that the bowstring is not plucked. It should be gently released. It is only too easy to allow the bowstring to roll forward, or 'creep', or to pull it back slightly so that the arrow is given some unwanted extra impetus. Most archers cultivate a 'follow through', keeping their bow arm at the horizontal and their string hand moving slowly back until the arrow is well on its way to the target.

Competitive archery. Once you can use a bow and arrow with confidence, you will want to try your skill on target archery.

If you join a club, you will probably be invited to shoot at a four-foot circular target, which will be mounted on a thick boss or backing, usually made of coiled straw. This, in turn, will be set on a wooden tripod base so that it hangs at 15° or so off the vertical, and so that the centre is 4 ft from the ground.

The face of the target will be clearly marked with concentric circles. If your arrow lands in the inmost circle, which is coloured gold, you will be awarded a score of nine. The next ring is red, and has a value of seven, and outside that come blue (five), black (three) and white (one).

The Grand National Archery Society prescribes certain 'rounds' that should be used for practice and for competition. To complete a 'York' round, for example, you have to shoot one hundred and forty-four arrows—seventy-two at a distance of one hundred yards, forty-eight at eighty yards, and the last twenty-four at sixty yards. If you can shoot three York rounds with a score on each round of 700 or better, you will qualify as a Master Bowman, which is one of the most difficult classifications to attain in any sport.

Further reading

EDMUND BURKE, *Archery* (Arco Publications).
HOWARD WISEMAN, *Tackle Archery This Way* (Stanley Paul).
GORDON GRIMLEY, *The Book of the Bow* (Putnam).
FRANK BILSON, *Bowmanship* (Country Life).

Astronomy

Human beings have always been fascinated by the sun, the moon, and the great canopy of stars that gleam over our heads by night, and are only effaced during the day by the greater brilliance of the empyrean. If you have ever marvelled at the beauty and complexity of the heavens you will find astronomy an intriguing hobby. It will help you to appreciate the marvellous work done at such great observatories as the Royal Greenwich, Mount Wilson and Jodrell Bank, too—research that is so vitally necessary in these days when space travel is rapidly becoming a commonplace, and the moon is no longer an unattainable dream.

Equipment. Buying or building an astronomical telescope of any kind is a great adventure that can involve the inexperienced amateur in a good deal—or bad deal—of trouble and expense. Fortunately, it is an adventure that can be postponed, as you can learn to find your way round the heavens quite well with the naked eye—and, in fact, you will probably enjoy your first steps in celestial exploration better if you don't have to worry about optical technicalities. The important thing is to start looking at the night sky with intelligent curiosity at every available opportunity.

Fortunately, there are some excellent guides on the market that will help you to find your way round the heavens at any time in the year.

Norton's Star Atlas, obtainable from Messrs George Philip and Son, 14 Long Acre, London, WC2, is one of the best known and most reliable.

An excellent Planisphere, or circular star map that you can rotate and set for any time, on any day of the month, can be obtained for a few shillings from Messrs George Philip and Son.

There is also much useful information to be found in *Whitaker's Almanack*, where the sun's declination, or angular distance north or south of the celestial equator is given for each day, together with other invaluable facts.

A visit to a Planetarium can be really informative and inspiring. There, you can see the movements of the sun, the planets and the stars reproduced and speeded up, so that a whole night's happenings can be compressed into a few minutes. The London Planetarium, in Baker Street, NW1, is the largest in the country. A smaller one, the Caid, has recently opened at the Greenwich Maritime Museum. There is another in South Shields.

The sun. The sun, our sun, is not the largest star by any means—there are stars many thousands of times larger and more luminous. But it does happen to matter more to us than any of the others, so it is only to be expected that its phenomena will attract the attention even of those people who are not particularly interested in astronomy.

Take sunspots, for instance. Large sunspots are sometimes so obvious that they can be seen, if the sun is near the horizon, with the naked eye. But don't be tempted to look straight at the sun unless it is shrouded with mist, or you may do serious damage to your eyes. It is more dangerous still to look at the sun through a telescope or binoculars, since a lens may all too easily act as a burning glass, and blind you. It is quite safe, however, to look at it through a piece of heavily smoked glass.

The moon. Even with the naked eye you can enjoy studying the surface of the earth's nearest neighbour in space, the moon. With a small telescope and a copy of Elger's *Map of the Moon*, published by George Philip and Son, you can have an exciting time exploring the mountains, valleys and 'maria', or great plains, on its visible face. The other face, of course, is always turned away from us.

The planets. The word 'planet' should only be applied, properly, to the celestial bodies which revolve about our sun, and which, with the earth, constitute what we call our 'solar system'. As far as we know, there are six *superior* planets—that is to say, planets whose orbits lie outside that of the earth:

Mars is a comparatively small planet that can be seen with the naked eye, and may sometimes be identified by its distinctive reddish light.

Jupiter can easily be seen without any optical aid—in fact, it can outshine all the stars and every other planet except Venus when that planet is at its brightest. If you have a telescope or a strong pair of binoculars you may be able to see one, two, three or four of Jupiter's largest satellites—Io, Europa, Ganymede and Callisto.

Saturn is so far from the earth that it is not much brighter than a first-magnitude star. Unfortunately, the system of rings that has made Saturn so famous cannot be seen without a telescope.

Uranus is not very bright, and if you have no telescope you may not be able to distinguish it from the stars that surround it. It seems to us, however, a very slow traveller (it takes more than eighty years to pass once round the sun) and so its position in the sky at any time can be easily discovered by reference to the British Astronomical Association's Handbook.

Pluto and *Neptune* are so remote that they were not discovered until comparatively recently (Neptune during the nineteenth century, Pluto in 1930). You are not likely to be much concerned with their movements unless you acquire a powerful telescope.

The two inferior planets, which revolve between the earth and the sun are:

34

Mercury, the planet nearest to the sun. It is difficult to see, except occasionally just before sunrise or just after sunset.

Venus, on the other hand, is extremely brilliant—so bright, that it can be seen on some clear moonless nights to cast shadows. Known occasionally as the 'Evening Star' and the 'Morning Star', Venus was called 'Hesperus' and 'Phosphorus' by ancient observers, who did not realize that the two luminous bodies they admired were, in fact, one and the same celestial orb.

There are also some minor planets, such as Ceres, Pallas, Juno and Vesta, but their movements may not interest you.

'Fixed' stars. This is the name usually given to the orbs which shine by their own light so brightly that as many as five thousand may be visible to the unaided eye at different times of the year.

The word 'fixed' is misleading, since they are all, in fact, travelling through space at very great rates—some at speeds that are beyond our power of mental measurement. To all intents and purposes, though, the stars that make up the various constellations remain in the same relative positions in the sky as the earth revolves upon its own axis.

The eight brightest stars, in the order of their brightness, are Sirius, Canopus, Alpha of the Centaur, Vega, Capella, Arcturus, and Rigel. Canopus and Alpha of the Centaur, being situate in the Southern Hemisphere, are not visible from Britain. You can find the others quite easily with the aid of *Norton's Star Atlas*.

Comets. Comets are very occasional visitors in the night sky, and as they travel enormous distances through outer space to reappear

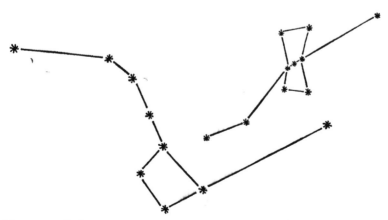

Two constellations

The Great Bear   Orion

35

at closely predictable intervals of time they usually attract a lot of public attention when they do come into our view.

About 3000 comets have been recorded in the past 2000 years, one of the most spectacular and noticeable being known as Halley's Comet. When this appeared in 1456, Turkish armies were ravaging many parts of Europe, and the comet and the Turks together were roundly rebuked by the Pope of that time, in a Papal Bull.

Halley's Comet last appeared in 1910, when the earth actually passed through its tail, and it should be with us again in 1986. But there will be other comets to be seen before then.

Meteors, or Shooting Stars, may be seen on almost any clear moonless night. They are particles of matter, some huge, some minute, which hurtle through space and occasionally penetrate the earth's atmosphere. If they are not completely burnt out in their flight through the atmosphere, they fall to the ground as meteorites. There are certain times of the year when they seem to appear in the very greatest profusion. One of these 'meteor showers' occurs every year during the last week of July and the first two weeks of August, when the *Perseid* meteors burn themselves out in the earth's outer atmosphere. Another splendid display is provided by the *Geminids* in mid-December, but by that time conditions may not be so good for meteor-watching out of doors!

Eclipses. All eclipses of the sun and moon, whether total or partial, excite professional astronomers, who can get a lot of valuable information by observing our best-known heavenly bodies under these unusual conditions. Fortunately for those people who have to treat astronomy merely as a hobby, the time, nature and duration of every eclipse can be exactly foretold, and there is always plenty of advance publicity in the Press.

Telescopes. If your interest in astronomy increases to the point where you cannot carry on happily without a telescope, you will find some useful information in the books mentioned in the list below.

Societies. You may like to consider joining one of these well-established societies:

The Royal Astronomical Society (Burlington House, Piccadilly, London, W1). Fellows and Junior Members. Has as its main object the encouragement and promotion of astronomy.

The British Astronomical Association (Registered Office: 303 Bath Road, Hounslow West, Middlesex). Fosters a popular interest in astronomy and keeps observers in touch for mutual help and information.

The Junior Astronomical Society (Hon. Secretary: E. W. Turner,

44 Cedar Way, Basingstoke, Hants). For all people, irrespective of age, who are taking their first steps in astronomy.

Further reading

KENNETH BAILEY, *Stars and Planets* (Studio Vista). (This is an elementary introduction.)

GUNTER D. ROTH, *The Amateur Astronomer and his Telescope* (Faber and Faber).

H. C. KING, *Astronomy* (Studio Vista).

H. C. KING, *Tackle Astronomy This Way* (Stanley Paul).

JAMES MUIRDEN, *Astronomy with Binoculars* (Faber and Faber).

PATRICK MOORE (Ed.), *Practical Amateur Astronomy* (Lutterworth).

Bird watching

There are birds in the sky, birds in the trees, birds on the ground, birds almost everywhere we look when we are out of doors. Even great cities like London have an exciting quota of resident birds and visiting migrants. It is not surprising that bird watching has become an extremely popular hobby with people who enjoy studying wild life, and like to be able to do so without having to travel long distances to game reserves and nature conservancies.

Equipment for bird watching. If your eyesight is good, you won't need any special equipment for bird watching except a notebook in which to record what you see. It is a help, however, to have a good pair of binoculars. The cost of any good optical aid may be considerable, so it is advisable to consult some experienced authority before you make any outlay. You may find helpful the British Trust for Ornithology Field Guide No. 2: *How to Choose and Use Field Glasses*, by J. R. Hebditch. It costs 1s., plus postage, and it is obtainable from the BTO, 2 King Edward Street, Oxford.

Identification. The amount of enjoyment you get from bird watching will depend to a large extent on your skill at identifying the birds you see and hear. Your aim should be to become so clever at this that you can dispense altogether with books, charts and guides. Until that happy day arrives, you may find these particularly helpful:

R. S. R. Fitter and R. A. Richardson, *The Pocket Guide to British Birds*, Collins.

R. Peterson, G. Mountford and P. A. D. Hollom, *A Field Guide to the Birds of Britain and Europe*, Collins.

Recognition is not only a matter of recording the relative size and characteristic plumage of the birds you see. Often, you will want to 'put a name to' a bird that you can only see in the distance—across a field, possibly, or out on some mud flats in an estuary. Then, you may be given the key to the puzzle by the way the bird flies—the Cuckoo's pendulous tail, for example, will always give it away—or by some peculiarity of its gait. After you have had a little experience, you should be able to identify without guess-work all the birds that are normally found in a neighbourhood. Then you will be free to look for rare visitors.

Your field notebook. This will become your principal aid to identification, if you keep it conscientiously. In it, you should make notes about the birds you have watched, and their behaviour, and you can put in it any sketches or photographs you feel competent to make or take. You can use it as a scrapbook, too, pasting into it any magazine articles, newspaper cuttings, maps, or charts that you think may be relevant. A loose leaf album is preferable to a permanently bound book, because you may want to add extra leaves when any species merits an extended entry.

Some bird watchers like to collect typical or exceptionally beautiful feathers. If you wish to put any in your field notebook, cover them with polythene or cellophane and seal down the edges with adhesive tape. This will protect them from the ravages of mites and moth grubs and other small destructive creatures.

Great Tit

Dartford Warbler

Starlings

Characteristics. Before you have been bird watching for long, you will find yourself becoming increasingly aware of the widely different behaviour patterns of the birds you are studying. Here are some of the special characteristics you should look for:

Flight. Notice whether the bird you have under observation is flapping, gliding, soaring or moving forward by any combination of these. If you are really observant, you will be able to tell when a bird is making use of upward air currents to gain height.

Courtship. Some birds stage elaborate courtship displays as the nesting season approaches. Their strange rituals should be carefully recorded.

Preening. A bird's feathers need to be preened regularly if the bird is to remain healthy and in good flying condition. Notice this and other instinctive habits, such as bathing and dust-bathing (dry cleaning is preferred by some birds to getting wet!).

Anting. Many birds will pick up ants and place them in their plumage. The reason for this action is not positively known. Have you ever seen it happening?

Territory holding. Rigid boundaries invisible to the human eye seem to separate the territories 'owned' and patrolled by the individual members of a resident bird community. Bird song, which is so justly admired, is closely bound up with territory holding. By doing a little detective work you may be able to chart the territory that supports any bird you are studying.

Nesting. Chaffinches, Goldcrests and Long-tailed Tits, and many other small birds, build beautifully contrived nests with thick soft comfortable linings made from hundreds of feathers. The Common Tern is content with a shallow depression in some dry shingle. Between those two extremes you can find so many different kinds of nest that whole books could be written about the possible variations. It is unfortunate, for bird watchers, that nesting takes place in a comparatively short season.

Migration. We cannot hope to understand the distribution of the birds in our hemisphere and the sudden disappearances and the equally sudden returns that make a bird watcher's life endlessly stimulating, unless we know a little about seasonal migration. What is the strange urge that can take a small Sedge Warbler from a reed bed in the north of England to winter in South Africa, and can bring it back exactly to its original territory? Or a Manx Shearwater from Skokholm, off the Welsh coast, to South America, or to Australia? How do these birds manage to navigate so successfully on their long and arduous journeys? Your researches, if you become a keen bird-watcher, may help to throw a little more light on a matter that is still wrapped in a certain amount of mystery. Read about the ringing of migratory birds, and about the extraordinary information that is obtained from these marked wanderers, in the books listed at the end of this chapter.

Bird sanctuaries. Bird observatories and nature conservancies are, obviously, first rate places for bird watching, not only because in them you will be able to follow your hobby in splendid conditions, but also because you are likely to meet fellow enthusiasts there, and you will learn a lot in congenial company. For information, write to:

The Field Studies Council
Ravensmead, Keston, Kent
or
The Council for Nature
41 Queen's Gate, London, SW7

The British Trust for Ornithology may also be able to help you.

Further reading
JAMES FISHER, *Watching Birds* (Collins).
F. MARTIN DUNCAN, *Wonders of Migration* (Sampson Low & Marston).
W. H. HUDSON, *A Hind in Richmond Park* (J. M. Dent).
THE LONDON NATURAL HISTORY SOCIETY, *Birds of the London Area* (Rupert Hart-Davis).

Brass rubbing

Many people prefer a walk or bicycle ride in the country to have some definite objective. If you enjoy purposeful journeys more than aimless wandering, why not take up, as a hobby, the study of memorial brasses? The search for examples will take you to places you have never been to before, you will meet all kinds of interesting people, and you will get much authentic information about men and women who lived a long time ago—and about their clothes, their armour, if they possessed any, their heraldic achievements and their pets. You will learn how to make some most decorative rubbings, too, though experts insist that this is the least important part of the pastime!

What brasses are. The urge to leave graphic memorials of themselves or their kinsfolk for posterity to see and revere affected many worthy citizens in the Middle Ages. Instead of having stone or alabaster monuments set up, many people ordered that engraved portraits should be carried out in flat sheets of metal—'brasses', these are usually called, but the term applied at the time to the most suitable alloy was 'latten', from *latta*, a thin board or plate. Modern research has shown that copper and zinc were the principal components of latten, with lead and tin usually present in very much smaller quantities. So much latten was imported from Cologne that it has sometimes been called 'Cullen plate', as if it has never been made anywhere else.

The earliest monumental brasses were produced during the first half of the thirteenth century, unfortunately, it is no longer possible to see the 'first brass ever', since that has gone the way of so many other precious brasses—into the melting pot, leaving only an empty recess to tell us of its shape. But there are some splendid brasses to be seen which date from the second half of the thirteenth century, notable examples being the memorials of Sir Richard de Burslingthorpe, at Burslingthorpe in Lincolnshire, Sir Roger de Trumpington, at Trumpington near Cambridge, and Sir John Daubernoun, at Stoke d'Abernon, in Surrey.

As soon as it became 'the thing' to commission sepulchral brasses, a thriving industry developed to satisfy the demand—centred, it seems, on London, York and Norwich. There, and at some places overseas, craftsmen wielded hammers and chisels with a rare combination of vigour and sensibility, producing bold designs that for purity of line and delicacy of detail have seldom, if ever, been excelled in the whole history of the Fine Arts.

Not all the brasses you see will have been produced from a single sheet of metal! In the Middle Ages, there was an outside limit on the size of the sheets of brass that could be produced in any foundry

—3ft × 3ft being the largest recorded. Memorial brasses larger than this would invariably be produced by brazing two standard-sized plates together, the joints being made so neatly that they are rarely perceptible.

Where to find brasses. Unfortunately, memorial brasses are not distributed at all evenly, and there are many districts where you will search for them in vain. You are most likely to be successful in the South of England and the Midlands; Kent, Sussex, Warwickshire, Norfolk and Shropshire being five counties where they are particularly plentiful. A few are to be found in Yorkshire, but generally speaking the extreme North of England is barren ground. There are barely half a dozen brasses in Scotland, and as few in Ireland.

Normally, a memorial brass will be set in the floor of a cathedral, abbey, church or chapel, or in the sanctuary steps of one of those buildings. Some brasses are set vertically, so that they become part of a wall surface. It is rather more difficult to take rubbings from these.

What to look for in brasses. Everyone who looks at memorial brasses will react in a different way—men and boys will probably notice armour, weapons and professional or trade symbols; women and girls will be much more aware of the vagaries of fashion. Here are some of the interesting features you may be unfortunate enough to miss, unless you are specially aware of them:

Military brasses. The full development of medieval military costume can be studied in memorial brasses, from the protective clothing or 'mail', made from links of chain, worn by the warriors of the time of Edward I, to the full plate armour worn by the Lancastrians and Yorkists, and the later Tudor refinements. Notice particularly the frequent use of the helmet, with its crest, as a pillow for the recumbent warrior.

Feminine fashions. The changes made in feminine attire over three eventful centuries can also be traced from memorial brasses. The head-dresses alone would make a most interesting study, varying as they do from the simple kerchiefs worn by the earliest subjects to the formal and richly decorated pediment head-dresses evolved for the ladies of the Tudor period.

Professional and trade emblems. It is often possible to tell the profession or trade of the person depicted in a memorial brass by some unobtrusive feature in the design. In Cirencester church, for instance, there is a brass that commemorates a fourteenth-century wine merchant. We know how he made his fortune, because his feet are resting on a tun or barrel.

Animals are shown in many brasses. A warrior's feet may be resting on a hound, a lion, or even an elephant. Ladies are often accompanied by minute but charming lapdogs.

Chrisoms. These are infants who failed to survive the first perilous weeks of medieval life. In memorial brasses they are shown so tightly wrapped that the poor little creatures look like tiny mummified Ancient Egyptians.

Cadavers. If you have a taste for the macabre you will enjoy finding the occasional brasses that show their subjects as skeletons, or being consumed by worms, or wrapped in a shroud!

Palimpsests. The plates used for memorial brasses were relatively expensive, and so waste had to be avoided. Occasionally, you will find 'palimpsest' brasses—so called, because the original engraving has been erased or altered in some way so that the brass can be used for commemorating a new subject. In rare cases a brass will be engraved on both sides. This may only be properly appreciated if the brass is fixed to a wall with hinges, so that it can swing. There is a brass of this kind in Salhouse church, near the Norfolk Broads.

How to take rubbings from brasses. If you see a brass that you would like to record, get permission from the clergyman in charge, or from his verger or sexton, or, failing these, from a churchwarden.

Next, get a brush with soft bristles—a clothes brush will do splendidly—and sweep away any dust or fluff that may have collected inside the incised lines.

Delightfully smooth papers—white, strong and thin—are sold by the roll specially for brass rubbing. These are more expensive than the shelf papers and kitchen papers sometimes recommended, but they will not have the same tendency to turn yellow as time elapses.

If the brass from which you wish to take a rubbing is set in a horizontal position you will be able to use kneeling hassocks or some other handy weights to hold the paper over it while you do the rubbing. If the brass is set in a wall, you may have to use narrow strips of Sellotape or some other self-adhesive material, but this is not to be recommended if it can possibly be avoided, as a slight tendency to stickiness is virtually certain to be left on the surrounding surface, and this will inevitably collect dirt.

With a stick of cobbler's wax or heel-ball you can reproduce on your paper the flat brass shapes with the greatest of ease. The wax will only darken the paper's surface where it has something firm to rest on. As the engraved parts of the plate will give the paper no support, a black and white facsimile will quickly appear. As you will no doubt appreciate, your brass rubbings may make magnificent mural decorations when you have got them home. Best results can be obtained from heel-ball sold by Phillips and Page Ltd, 50 Kensington Church Street, London, W8.

Further reading
Julian Franklyn, *Brasses* (Arco Publications).
Malcolm Norris, *Brass Rubbing* (Studio Vista).
Sir James Mann, *Monumental Brasses* (Penguin).
H. W. Macklin, *Monumental Brasses* (Allen & Unwin) (contains county lists of extant brasses).

Butterfly and moth hunting

This section has been called 'Butterfly and Moth Hunting' rather than 'Collecting Butterflies and Moths' because nowadays the number of people who enjoy catching and killing these defenceless and beautiful little creatures is definitely fewer. Many people believe that no butterflies or moths should be killed at all, for recreational purposes, since so many of them are being destroyed by the poisonous sprays used by farmers, fruit growers and nurserymen. On the other hand, the number of people who are eager to find and study butterflies and moths in their natural surroundings is steadily increasing. There are few hobbies more delightful than 'entomology', though entomology, properly speaking, includes all insects.

What is a butterfly? The name 'Lepidoptera' is used by scientists to describe all butterflies and moths, which are really four-winged insects of a very special kind. Their uniqueness lies chiefly in the structure of their wings, which are covered with beautiful scales too small to be appreciated properly by the naked eye, but they have other features which make them of very great interest to the naturalist. Do you know, for instance:

That a butterfly or moth which has lost its antennae or feelers will not be able to fly properly because it will have lost its sense of balance? And that it will have been deprived of its extraordinarily acute sense of smell?

That a butterfly or moth has four eyes, two of which are large and fantastically complex? Micro-photographs reveal that each of these compound eyes is made up of several thousand minute hexagonal lenses or facets.

That no butterfly or moth has a proper 'mouth', as we understand that term? Instead, each insect has a long hollow trunk, or 'haustellum', that it can uncoil when it wants to imbibe liquid nourishment. Between feeds, this pipe is rolled away neatly under its head like a watch-spring.

That some butterflies migrate?

If you don't know whether you are looking at a butterfly or a moth, look closely at the antennae. In butterflies, these are always distinctly clubbed at the tip. Some moths have antennae with slightly swollen ends, but none have marked protuberances, as have all butterflies.

The life cycle of butterflies and moths. Although there are hundreds of different species of butterflies and moths waiting to be found and identified by you, each species will pass through exactly the same life cycle, though the members of that species may behave during any one of the four separate stages in a highly distinctive way. The stages are:

The egg. Most butterflies and moths lay their eggs only on their foodplants. The eggs of the different species vary widely in shape, size, colour and texture, some being as magnificently formed or marked as the most significant works by outstanding artists. To appreciate their beauties fully you will need access to a microscope.
The larva. When the infant larva is ready to hatch, it eats (or pushes) its way out through the shell of its egg and emerges as a caterpillar. Its chances of life during the next few days are usually extremely precarious—it may starve, it may be eaten by one of its fellows, or it may be devoured by a bird or by one of its many other natural enemies. If it survives, it will go through a number of moults or changes of skin, the last one of which will produce
The pupa or chrysalis. There are many different ways in which an embryonic butterfly or moth may spend the period of time known as 'pupation'. Some caterpillars, such as those of the Orangetip and Brimstone butterflies, attach themselves to a stem of their foodplant with a silken girdle. Others spin a complete cocoon. Many bury themselves in the ground. It may be months or even years before
The mature and nearly perfect insects are ready to emerge. When that time comes, the skin of the pupa splits, and the *imago*, with limp and crumpled wings, crawls out. It may be an hour before the insect is ready to fly, this brief period of transformation being one of the most interesting to study in the whole process of growth.

Where to find butterflies and moths. Butterflies and moths are strangely consistent in their choice of places to live and breed, and it is not often much use looking for (say) a Swallowtail butterfly in a part of the country that Swallowtails have never been known to visit, or a woodland butterfly such as a Purple Hairstreak out on the open downs. You will soon find out which species are habitually found in the district in which you live, or which you are visiting, and which lanes, gardens, meadows, hollows and woodland clearings they prefer. You will be helped by a knowledge of botany, for most butterflies and moths have their own favourite foodplants, and do not take kindly to substitutes.

Nets. If you really want to make a collection of butterflies and moths, you will need a net.

There are several types to choose from, folding nets being particularly favoured by lepidopterists who have to travel long distances to their hunting grounds.

It is important to see that the netting bag is made from some really soft fine material such as gauze or linen, and that it is deep enough to allow a proper turnover (captured insects can quickly escape from shallow nets). See that the ends and corners are gently rounded too, to prevent damage to the fragile occupants.

It is easier to see butterflies and moths through dark nets than through light ones. If the only nets offered to you are made from white muslin or gauze you may be able to dip one in black or dark green dye and dry it out thoroughly before you go out hunting.

Net handles should be light and strong, but they do not have to be particularly long unless you intend to sweep most of your specimens from around street lamps or the tops of trees! Normally, you should be able to approach a butterfly or moth so that it is well within arm's length.

A killing bottle. This should be wide-mouthed, so that you can get the insects into it quickly and easily. A tightly fitting cork makes a good bung. Alternatively, a clean screw-top pickle jar can be used. The poisons most often used for killing bottles are:

Cyanide of Potassium. This is quite deadly, and can only be obtained from chemists, if the most stringent safeguards are complied with (the poison book has to be signed, incidentally, to conform with the Dangerous Drugs Act). The white crystals are usually placed on the bottom of a killing bottle and then covered with liquid plaster of paris. This hardens, but allows the fumes to fill the bottle for quite a number of years.

Ammonia. Only solid ammonia (ammonium carbonate) or the strongest concentration of liquid ammonia (usually called '880') sprinkled on to blotting paper should be used. Isolate the insects from the ammonia with a layer of clean cotton wool. Ammonia has a tendency to discolour some specimens, especially if they are left in the fumes for too long.

Ethyl acetate. A few drops of this introduced into a killing bottle on blotting paper or a plaster of paris floor will usually be quite effective.

Laurel leaves, chopped up finely and crushed, can also be used, but the fumes they produce may be very slow in taking effect.

Unless they are very adequately anaesthetized, butterflies and moths are liable to come to life and start fluttering again long after they seem to be dead. This can be rather disconcerting for the normally humane collector.

Relaxing. Before a recently killed butterfly or moth can be set in the position it is to occupy permanently, it must be allowed or encouraged to relax. Insects killed with ammonia need little or no relaxation time; those killed in cyanide bottles undergo a period of *rigor mortis* which may last for as much as thirty-six hours.

If you want to speed the process of relaxation (or if you want to make more amenable some insects that have already started to harden) leave your specimens in a damp atmosphere for a short time.

A metal box lined with cork sheet makes an excellent 'relaxing case'. Pour a little boiling water on the cork, shake away the surplus fluid, and pin the insects so that they do not touch the damp surface. Then close the lid tightly and leave the box for an hour or two—but do not forget that the insects are there, or they may go mouldy!

Pinning. Ordinary household pins can be used for setting butterflies and moths, but the special black pins prepared for entomologists give a collection a really professional look. They can be obtained in a number of different sizes to suit all kinds of insects.

To pin a butterfly or moth, hold it carefully between the forefinger and thumb of your left hand (if you are right-handed) and then insert the point of the pin exactly in the middle of the thorax (that is, the 'leggy' part of the body). Then push the pin through, so that the point emerges between the second pair of legs and the third pair. If you do this correctly, the pin will slant so that its head is slightly forward of the point. You will find a pair of curved forceps extremely useful when carrying out this decidedly tricky operation.

Setting. Special grooved setting boards can be bought at all shops that sell equipment for naturalists, but you can make your own quite easily by gluing some strips of sheet cork to a piece of plywood, or, alternatively, by joining some pieces of balsa wood with balsa cement. To set a butterfly, place its body in the groove in the middle of the setting board, and then drive the pin carefully home so that the wings rest lightly on the flat surfaces to each side.

You may find the job of moving the wings, the antennae, and the legs into really natural positions much easier if you can guide them

49

carefully with a fine needle (push it through a cork, if you need a handle) or a hoghair bristle. As soon as you are satisfied with the relative positions of the wings, fix them carefully with narrow strips of transparent paper or greaseproof paper or with small triangles of thin smooth card. You may need a little bit of practice before you can carry out this ticklish operation without damaging the incredibly delicate membranes of your precious specimens.

You will be able to obtain all the equipment you need from Messrs. Watkins and Doncaster, 110 Park View Road, Welling, Kent. If you do not live in this area you may take advantage of their mail-order service.

Display. Leave all specimens on the setting board in a dry, dust-free mouse-proof place for several weeks before you remove them. Then you will have to provide some kind of a case for them that will allow you to inspect them whenever you want to, without allowing mites or museum beetles to get at them, to wreak their work of destruction. Fortunately, there are several good insecticides on the market nowadays, with any one of which all display cases should periodically be dusted.

Further reading
IAN HARMAN, *Collecting Butterflies and Moths* (Williams and Norgate).
RICHARD SOUTH, *The Butterflies of the British Isles* (Frederick Warne).
RICHARD SOUTH, *The Moths of the British Isles* (Frederick Warne).

Camping

As the civilized world becomes more crowded, the popularity of camping increases. It is a hobby that offers us a delightful feeling of adventure, the chance to get away from our familiar surroundings, and opportunities to travel cheaply. It enables us to meet people, and to make new friends in an atmosphere of carefree informality that would be out of place in a hotel or boarding house. No wonder more people are setting off on camping holidays every year!

If you have never been camping before, you will probably be wondering if the equipment will be very expensive. The answer to that question depends upon your resources, and the amount of comfort you are going to find necessary. Young people are usually hardy enough to be able to get around with a minimum of lightweight equipment, and versatile enough to be able to find or improvise additional shelter when weather conditions are particularly unpleasant. Older people are often happier with spacious, well-fitted tents, and with the sort of comforts they are used to at home. Campers of all kinds are more than adequately catered for nowadays by manufacturers and retailers, and there are several organizations that you can join if you need advice and up-to-date information about camping sites. These are described in more detail on pages 58 and 59.

Tents. To enjoy camping to the full, you will need to sleep properly at night, and you will not be able to do this unless you are warm and dry. Whatever type of tent you decide to buy, you will have to make sure that it will afford you adequate protection from rain and wind, and—this is very important—complete insulation between yourself and the ground. Cold can strike upwards in the small hours and make a night seem very long and miserable!

First, make sure that your tent is going to be large enough. If it is so low and so narrow that you cannot avoid touching the walls or

the roof you will probably bring moisture inside by capillary attraction. A tent fitted with a flysheet will not be prone to this inconvenience. The flysheet acts as an extra roof, and will help to insulate the tent when the sunshine is uncomfortably hot, besides providing additional space for storage.

Then see that the tent has complete groundsheet coverage. Some tents are fitted with sewn-in groundsheets, and many people prefer these because they are draught-proof, insect-proof, and virtually watertight. On the other hand, a separate groundsheet is easier to clean and dry. And, if it wears out, you can replace it without having to do away with the rest of the tent.

These are some of the tents you may be offered. As your choice will be affected by your mode of travel, the lighter, more easily transported tents are placed first in the list:

Single pole tents are always popular with pedestrian campers because they are among the lightest made. Blacks' 'Good Companion' Minor, for example, weighs a little over 4 lb, yet will accommodate two people comfortably. Complete with a double-sided PVC fabric groundsheet and a flysheet the whole load is less than 9 lb. Terylene tents can be obtained that weigh even less than this, but if you choose one of these you may have to be prepared for the effects of condensation.

Some single pole tents are made with the pole forked so that it looks like an inverted V. The tent is then suspended in the space between the arms of the V, and the floor area can be unbroken. Unfortunately, tents of this kind weigh more than tents with one straight pole and they are more vulnerable to damage by high winds.

Cottage tents may be considerably heavier than the single pole tents designed for the walker or cyclist, but they have high walls —some as much as 3 ft—and, therefore, provide plenty of space for movement. The best cottage tents have flysheets, and walls that can be rolled up from time to time when the tent and the ground it covers need an airing.

Frame tents are obtainable in a wide variety of shapes and sizes, and some models are remarkably commodious, providing a 'room' for living and plenty of space for sleeping and cooking, as well as facilities for attaching extensions, such as a bathroom or a sun verandah. The fabric is stretched over a tubular metal frame, and this is specially designed so that the tent can be erected or packed away after a little practice in a very few minutes. The only disadvantage of frame tents lies in their bulkiness and their weight— they are definitely intended for motorist campers, and not for ramblers.

There are other tents on the market, beside those mentioned here— 'igloo' tents, for example, that are supported by a framework of inflatable rubber tubes, and the tents designed specially for use on windswept mountain ledges. Don't decide on any one type until you have had a chance to examine a good selection—if you can, visit one of the great comprehensive displays arranged for campers, such as the 'Camping and Outdoor Life' Exhibition held each year at Olympia, London.

Sleeping bags. You won't want to be bothered with a lot of sheets and blankets when you go camping—it is better to invest in a warm, light sleeping bag that can be packed away into a relatively small space. If you are only planning to camp out occasionally, and then only for the odd night or two in the summer, you can make do with a cheap felt- or kapok-filled bag, but if you intend to go 'under canvas' for longer spells you will be more comfortable in a bag filled with down or Terylene.

Down bags are still popular, and can be bought in many different shapes and sizes. They are not very easy to wash, so it is best to fit them with detachable linings.

Terylene-filled bags are a little more expensive, but they are comfortable, warm, easily washed and obtainable in some very decorative covers. The best Terylene-filled bags can be converted into splendid bed quilts when they are not needed for camping, and this saves storage space, as well as providing extra home bedding.

To isolate yourself from the ground at night you may be able to use some extra item of equipment to supplement your groundsheet. Folding camp beds are only to be recommended if you are going to your camping ground by car, but inflatable airbeds are rather more portable, and will last quite a long time as long as they are always inflated with a pump (blowing them up with your mouth will introduce moisture into the interior) and protected from strong sunlight, salt water, and, of course, pins and thorns. If an airbed does get punctured, it can be repaired with an adhesive rubber patch, exactly as the inner tube of a flat bicycle tyre is mended.

Cooking. The word 'camping' brings to many young people's minds the excitement of cooking and eating meals out of doors, round a wood fire, with primitive utensils, and with the acrid smell of smoke as an appetizer. Unfortunately, open fire cooking, though romantic, is not often practicable, and on most camp sites it is definitely not allowed.

So, if you want to prepare food quickly and conveniently when you are camping, you will have to take a cooking stove of some kind with you. There are several excellent types from which to choose. Here are a few suggestions:

Paraffin stoves are very popular. If you decide to use one, you will need methylated spirits (either liquid or solidified) for the initial priming, as well as an adequate supply of fuel. You will have to learn how to fill and light the stove too, but clear instructions are usually given by the manufacturers. A pressure pump is incorporated that will help the stove to provide really intensive heat.

Petrol stoves are sometimes preferred to paraffin stoves because they do not need methylated spirits for priming. On the other hand, the highly inflammable nature of petrol gives them a distinct element of danger and they should be used, if at all, with the utmost care.

Methylated spirits stoves are much safer, but it is not possible to produce a very intense heat with them.

Gas stoves are safe, easy to use, and efficient. You just have to turn a tap and light the gas, as with many domestic cookers. Their only disadvantage from the camper's point of view is their weight, and in particular the weight of the gas containers. This makes them unsuitable for use on rambling or cycling holidays. If you are able to carry your camping equipment by car, you should be able to take enough gas with you for quite a long holiday, in two 10 lb or 12 lb containers.

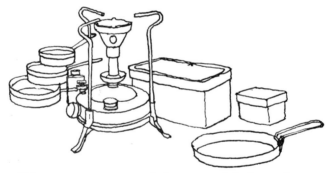

Primus stove, saucepans, frying pan and food containers

Other equipment. Before you set off on a camping holiday, take a pen or pencil and a piece of paper and make a list of all the pieces of equipment you are likely to need while you are away. No two lists will be alike, but here are some of the items that should definitely be included:

A container for water. It is annoying to have to search for a supply of fresh water whenever you want to have a meal, or to make a cup of tea, so wise campers take water with them, using one of the canvas, polythene or plasticized buckets or bottles manufactured specially for the purpose, or making use of one of the excellent containers in which liquids of various kinds are marketed nowadays.

A washing bowl. The round plastic bowls sold for a shilling or two at all household stores are quite adequate.

54

Saucepans, a kettle and a frying pan, according to your requirements. *Plastic containers,* obtainable at any household stores, for food and condiments. It is possible to buy portable larders that fold flat for packing and then can be hung from a tree or a post when needed for storage. Insulated bags and thermos flasks are useful if you are going to camp in very cold or very warm conditions.

Cutlery. Don't take the best knives, forks and spoons from home, as small implements can so easily get lost when meals are prepared and devoured out of doors. It is better to buy a replaceable supply of cheap cutlery from a chain store.

A refuse container. To enjoy camping to the full you must be methodical and tidy, and it will help if you can take with you a container large enough to hold your refuse until you find a suitable way to dispose of it.

A needle and thread, for emergency repairs to clothing. There are a lot of small miscellaneous items such as clothes pegs and safety pins that you can usefully include in your baggage if you can carry them without inconvenience.

Kit for first aid. However conscientiously you try to avoid accidents when you are camping, it is always useful to have a simple First Aid kit with you, for cuts and scratches are liable to result from vigorous activity in strange surroundings, and the ill effects of these can be minimized if they are dealt with properly, and without delay. In a small tin or cardboard box you could pack:

A small bottle of a good antiseptic (any chemist will recommend one that is generally useful).
Some adhesive dressings, or 'Elastoplast'.
A bandage or two.
Some cotton wool.
Boracic powder.
A needle, for extracting thorns and splinters.
A small bottle of ammonia.
A pair of scissors.

A daily foot inspection is advisable when you are doing a lot of walking. Dust your feet regularly with boracic powder if you want to avoid blisters. If, in spite of this precaution, a blister appears, prick it with a sterilized needle (hold the point for a second or two in a match flame to remove all danger of infection). Then squeeze the fluid out of the blister with a little cotton wool, dab some antiseptic over the spot, and protect it with one of your adhesive dressings.

Bee stings and wasp stings can also be troublesome when you are spending a lot of time out of doors. If you are unfortunate enough to be stung by a bee, you will probably find that it has left the barbed end of its sting behind in your flesh. Extract this as quickly as you can with your fingers, a needle, or a split match stick, and then dab a solution of ammonia (to neutralize the acid left by the bee) freely over the spot. A wasp is not likely to leave any part of its sting in you, but it will leave a strong solution of alkali behind. To neutralize this you can use any safe, homely acid such as lemon juice or vinegar.

The only poisonous snake to be found in Britain is the adder, which can usually be identified by the zigzag markings it bears on its back. Fortunately, an adder bite is a very rare catastrophe, but it is one that must be dealt with by a doctor, and quickly too. As an emergency measure, you can try to suck as much as possible of the venom away, and spit it out, but this is not a substitute for proper medical attention. If you can spare the time for a recognized course in First Aid before you go camping you will be in a better position to cope, temporarily, with any other mishaps that may occur.

Choosing a camping site. The more popular camping becomes, the harder it is to find places to camp in that are at once secluded and convenient. Some people do not mind pitching a tent in a crowded, organized site as long as it has plenty of 'civilized' amenities. If you would prefer to be all on your own, there are a few factors you will have to bear in mind if you want your holiday to be really enjoyable, and if you want to be popular with the people whose territory you are visiting:

Permission. You should always ask permission from the owner of the land before you pitch your tent. If it is impossible to find the owner—as, for example, on wild mountains or moorland—you are not likely to cause any offence if you camp out without authority for only one night. On all ordinary cultivated and semi-cultivated ground you must obtain the consent of the owner or occupier or you will almost certainly be a source of annoyance. Don't be shy about approaching farmers. Occasionally you will find yourself coolly received by someone who has suffered from inconsiderate campers before, but, more often, if you are quiet, unobtrusive and polite you will be told any drawbacks about the place you have chosen, and, if the drawbacks are insuperable (as, for example, when an untrustworthy bull is to use the field) you may well be offered a better site.

Suitable ground. Look closely at the ground before you choose the exact spot on which to pitch your tent. If the ground seems porous and well drained—as, for instance, when it is predominantly chalk, gravel or sand—it will probably not become waterlogged even when there is a prolonged downpour. Heavy clay, on the other hand, may make a moist foundation for a camp, even if you dig special drainage trenches. Be guided by the length of the grass— long lush grass usually betrays dampness, short wiry grass usually proclaims dryness!

Shelter. It may be very tempting to place your tent on an exposed piece of ground, where there is a fine view, but strong winds rising unexpectedly may easily make such a position uncomfortable or even untenable. Look ahead, therefore, and choose a pitch where the lie of the ground, or trees, or a hedge, or a wall will provide some shelter from the prevailing wind. It is not advisable to pitch a tent right under trees, though, as drips from the branches may bring unwanted acids and bugs down on to the fabric, as well as making a most disturbing noise.

The Country Code. All campers should study the Country Code, which has been compiled by the National Parks Commission. It is published by HM Stationery Office, and copies of it, price 6d, can be obtained from all branches of HMSO. Here are some of the most important pieces of advice contained in the pamphlet:

Guard against all risk of fire. The danger of fire cannot be over-stressed, especially after a dry spell. Many fires are traceable to matches and cigarette-ends carelessly thrown down, to broken bottles left to act as burning glasses in the sun, and to stoves lit too near dry crops or stacks. Children should not be allowed to play with matches. A match can set a rick alight in a moment.

If you discover a fire try to stamp it out, but if this is impossible report it to the fire brigade or the police at once.

Fasten all gates. Animals are naturally curious and will stray if gates are left open. They may stray far, they may harm themselves or cause accidents on the road and they may damage crops. They may eat too much or poison themselves or, in the case of tuberculin tested cattle, break their TT record by association with other cattle that have not been attested.

The farmer maintains his hedges and fences for the sake of his crops and livestock and is obliged by law to keep his animals in enclosed fields to safeguard them, his neighbours and the public.

All gates, even those found open, should be properly shut and fastened.

Keep dogs under proper control. More damage is done to farm animals by dogs than by any other single cause. Even friendly dogs which chase animals for fun cause a great deal of harm. Sheep suffer most, particularly in the breeding season, but cows are more easily frightened than most people realize and may lose a calf or give less milk if chased. Poultry may be put off laying and wild birds and game may lose their broods. Whether on farmland or mountain, if there are farm animals of any kind, dogs should be kept under close control and, if necessary, put on a lead.

Keep to paths across farmland. Crops are easily damaged (if they are trampled on) at any stage of growth; so are young plants and trees. Grown crops which are laid by walking or sitting may be awkward and costly to harvest. This is true of standing grass or hay too. So walk in single file across field paths, thus avoiding damage and (most important) keeping the path well defined.

Avoid damage to fences, hedges and walls. If you make a hole in a fence or a hedge or knock down a wall, animals can stray after you. There are gates and stiles to every field, and they should be used. If you can't open a gate, and if you must climb over it, climb over at the hinge side, to avoid unnecessary strain.

Leave no litter. Litter is unsightly and sometimes dangerous. Broken glass or tins often cause injury to cattle, sheep and horses; sheepdogs suffer cut paws too. Tins or bottles in fields may damage farm machinery. In ditches, streams or drains, litter can interfere with land drainage. If you must leave it behind, bury it deep—but, better still, take your litter home.

Safeguard water supplies. Many country people are still dependent on wells and streams for themselves and their animals. You wouldn't wash dishes or bathe in someone else's water supply or foul it in any way at home, so avoid doing it in the country. Campers should make proper arrangements for washing and sanitation and should not interfere in any way with cattle troughs, nor foul springs, streams or wells.

There are various ways in which you can ensure that your camping techniques are in no way offensive. For privacy, you can use a separate toilet tent, which need not be expensive or difficult to carry. A plastic chemical closet (if one can be transported) will cut out the need for trench digging. Concentrated disinfectants will keep the less public parts of your camp fragrant and free from flies and insects.

Camping in wet weather. Even an exciting stretch of country may seem dull and depressing when the rain starts to pour down relentlessly, so don't forget to include an interesting book in your camping equipment, and a pack of cards or a pocket chess set if they appeal to you. Adequate lighting will help you to while long evenings away without feeling bored—you can use a pressure lamp, of the 'hurricane' type, if you are really careful, or an electric lantern with long life batteries. Small, neat, portable fluorescent lights can now be obtained. Each has a 60-W tube, approximately 10 in. long, in a holder with a reflector and guard, and runs off a 12-volt car battery. Never be tempted to use ordinary candles when you go camping unless you have a safe lamp to put them in.

Camping associations. You can get up-to-date information about camping equipment and camping sites by joining one of the associations that cater specially for the outdoor holiday-maker. Best known of these is the Camping Club of Great Britain and Ireland, 11 Lower Grosvenor Place, London, SW1. Young people up to the age of eighteen may join a special branch of this club, The Camping Club

Youth. The membership is 5/- a year, plus 1/- entrance fee. There are also the following specialist groups within the club:

Association of Cycle Campers
British Caravanners' Club
Canoe Camping Club
Folk Dance and Song Group
Motor Caravanners' Section
Mountaineering Section
Photographic Section

Other bodies that may interest you are the Motor Caravanners' Club, 21 Shere Road, London, SE8, and the Youth Camping Association of Great Britain and Ireland, 38 Elmdale Road, Palmers Green, London, N13.

Canoeing

For those who can swim, and who enjoy physical pursuits out of doors, in lovely surroundings, canoeing makes a splendid hobby. If you are tempted to try it, you can buy a canoe ready made, or you can build one yourself, according to your interest in handicrafts. In either case, the cost of canoeing will seem small, when compared to the great pleasure the ownership of one of these light, handy craft will give you. An expedition in which canoeing is combined with camping can be one of the most economical holidays it is possible to plan, as well as being one of the most exciting.

How to start. If it is possible to do so, you should join one of the canoe clubs that are now thriving so successfully in most parts of the world. Certainly, there is no better way of finding out about canoes and canoeing—unless you are prepared to go on one of the special courses organized by the Central Council of Physical Recreation and similar bodies. You will learn more from a day's practical instruction than you will from months of theoretical study and bookwork. Here are some useful addresses:

The British Canoe Union,
147a Station Road, London, E4.

Most of the canoe clubs in Great Britain are affiliated to the BCU, and you will be able to find out from the Headquarters of the Union how to get in touch with your local enthusiasts.

The Canoe Camping Club,
11 Lower Grosvenor Place, London, SW1.

The Canoe Camping Club is a specialist group within the Camping Club of Great Britain and Ireland. If you join, you will be able to get up to date advice and many benefits. You will enjoy receiving copies of *Camping and Outdoor Life*, too. This is the monthly magazine of the Camping Club, and is issued free to members.

The Central Council of Physical Recreation,
26-29 Park Crescent, London, W1.

The officials of the CCPR will tell you where, and how, you can learn to become an expert canoeist under their auspices.

Your choice of canoes. All double-ended craft that are light enough to be propelled by paddles may be called 'canoes', but there are certain types that have been proved more suitable than others for touring and general purposes.

The question of length has to be considered at an early stage. A short 11 ft–12 ft single seater canoe will have a tendency to 'yaw' or

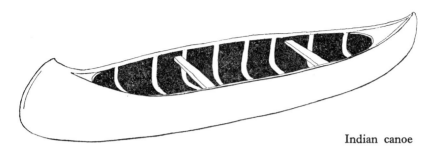

Indian canoe

change its direction slightly with the thrust given by each paddle stroke. A long 17 ft–18 ft single-seater canoe will keep on its set course with greater consistency, but it will not be so easy to manoeuvre. Somewhere between the two extremes there is a measurement that will be ideal for the beginner who wants to travel by canoe for enjoyment's sake, and not to win races. You will not go far wrong with a single-seater touring canoe that is 13 ft to 15 ft long with a 26-in. or 27-in. beam.

Generally speaking, a 'Canadian' or 'Red Indian' canoe is one with a comparatively broad beam. It is open-decked, and is usually propelled by a paddle with a single blade. There are obvious advantages in having a canoe of this type—it will be both relatively stable, and roomy—but it will not provide covered storage space for camping equipment so its uses for holiday purposes are limited.

The word 'kayak' was at one time used to describe any canoe with a rigid deck that could be propelled with a double-bladed paddle, or paddles. Now that canoeing is a popular and highly organized sport, the word 'kayak' is kept for the light and speedy craft of the type used for seal-hunting by the Eskimos, and in Greenland. These tend to be long and narrow and rather difficult to handle, and they are definitely not to be recommended for beginners.

Canoes may be constructed so that they will remain rigid, or so that they may be dismantled and folded away when they are not in use. If you are going to try constructing canoes in your own home workshop begin with a rigid, fabric-covered canoe. This will cost you less than a folding canoe, it will be much easier to make, and if it is a little harder to transport than a folding canoe this will be more than compensated for by its general convenience. The re-assembly of a folding canoe can seem a wearisome chore when you are eager to start out on a journey.

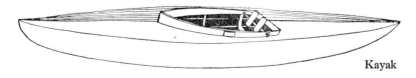

Kayak

Paddles. It is important to have a paddle that is properly adjusted to the type of canoe you are going to use. The longer a paddle is, the greater will be its tendency to turn a canoe with each separate thrust and the less will be its propulsive power. This sounds as if one should say 'the shorter the better', but unfortunately there are limits—you will not find it possible to use a paddle comfortably unless you can keep the blade clear of the side of the craft without your having to lean over too far. If you are using an ordinary touring canoe you will need a paddle about 8 ft long, though you may manage with a 7 ft paddle when you graduate to a narrow racing canoe.

Left Kayak, using single paddle *Right* Double-bladed paddle

Ready-made paddles can be bought at all shops that sell boating equipment. They are usually made of spruce, or spruce and mahogany. If you decide to make your own paddles at home, construct each in such a way that the loom (or central shaft) extends for the full length of the blade, so that the ridge acts as a strengthener. The tip or outmost edge of a blade should always be reinforced with a strip of copper plate or some suitable alloy, to prevent damage to this vulnerable part.

Spray covers. Even if you are a good swimmer, and don't mind getting wet, you will probably enjoy a long canoe journey more if you can manage to keep comparatively dry. A spray cover is, therefore, highly desirable. There are several types to choose from, most of which are held in place with elastic bands. Make sure that the type you choose will enable you to free yourself at once in an emergency. It is a good idea to practise a little 'self help' drill before you use a spray cover in rigorous conditions.

Other equipment. Once you have bought, or made, a canoe, a paddle and a spray cover you will be able to take to the water without much further outlay. Here are some items of equipment that may be helpful, but are not absolutely essential:

Painters. These are thin ropes used for general handling purposes, and may be attached to the framework of a canoe by means of small brass hooks or eyes. It is useful to be able to keep possession of a canoe, in an emergency, by seizing a painter that runs from bow to stern.

Paddle clips. A small bracket attached to the framework of your canoe may be extremely useful for holding your paddle when you have no 'spare hands'. It is rarely safe to leave a paddle lying loosely on the deck. Putting it down on the nearest piece of bank may be even more disastrous.

Pennants. Most canoe clubs have a distinguishing pennant. If you join such a club, you will be proud to fly its pennant at the bows of your canoe.

Canoeing clothes. Three conditions have to be satisfied by the clothes you choose for canoeing—they must keep you warm enough, they must allow you to move your limbs freely, and they must not interfere with your chances of reaching safety if you capsize. The claims of fashion will seem unimportant when you are afloat.

Life jackets are insisted on in some competitive canoeing events, but it does not necessarily follow that a life jacket designed for sailing will be suitable for use in a canoe. If you can find a life jacket that is at once buoyant enough to keep you afloat in difficult water, compact enough to take up little extra room in a touring canoe, and planned so that you can paddle for long periods of time without any discomfort, you may find it a worthwhile investment for the feeling of extra security it gives.

In fine weather, you will find it difficult to improve on light, informal garments such as short-sleeved shirts and short trousers. Long trousers and stockings are unsuitable because they are liable to get wet and stay wet. Corduroy, leather and similar materials that absorb water readily should be avoided. In cold wet weather a lightweight anorak will give you extra protection.

Footwear, too, should be chosen with care. Shoes that are likely to fill with water and remain undrained should be avoided. Rubber beach shoes are particularly unsuitable. Light plimsolls are excellent, and so are plastic sandals.

Getting waterborne. With a little practice, you will soon find it quite easy to launch a canoe of normal size, even if you have no one to help you.

To avoid damage, take particular care when you are lowering your canoe into the water and when you are getting it out. A canoe is rarely harmed by water, but hard ground can strain and tear. So, don't slide your canoe into the water even, but lift it by grasping the coaming at the point of balance.

When you have raised the canoe, rest it for a moment against your knees or thigh to steady it, and then lower the stern towards the water. As the end of the canoe becomes waterborne, move your hands towards the bows, grasping the gunwales if that grip is more convenient.

When lifting your canoe out of the water, reverse the process and raise the bows first. Then move your hands to the point of balance. Holding the canoe there, you will find the lift quite manageable.

If you have anyone to help you, you should stand with the canoe between you, and then you should each grasp the side of the coaming that is nearest to you. After that, you can raise the canoe and lower it into the water in the way just recommended for solo handling.

Stepping into a canoe is not easy, especially when you are getting into it from a high bank. To keep the craft as stable as possible, see that your weight is distributed evenly along the centre line of the canoe, and it helps if you can keep your weight as low as possible. It is unwise to stand up in a canoe if you can manage to sit down.

Paddling. A skilful waterman will be able to make a canoe move more swiftly than an inexperienced person, with considerably less effort. Here are some points that may help you to become fully proficient as quickly as possible:

Holding the paddle. Don't have your hands too close together when you grip the shaft. You should be able to sit comfortably in a space as wide as the gap between them.

Sharing the thrust. Each stroke of the paddle should be as long as you can comfortably make it, and the work should be shared by both arms. To ensure a steady and economic rhythm, keep your body as upright as possible, and make each stroke by thrusting forward with one arm while you pull the active blade backwards with the other.

Saving energy. Don't immerse the paddle blade too deeply in the water, and take some pains, when you are learning, to move it so that it just clears the coaming. You may make many hundreds of strokes in the course of quite a short journey. Each must be designed to produce as powerful an effect as possible from a minimum expenditure of energy.

To stop your canoe, make a number of quick reverse strokes, in which the paddle blade is moved forwards instead of backwards, on each side of the craft. Don't plunge the blade too deeply into the water until the canoe has lost a lot of its impetus.

Capsizing. If you go canoeing in a craft you can manage, on waters that present few unseen difficulties, you should be able to complete a great many journeys without being in any danger of capsizing. (A racing canoe cannot be as stable as an ordinary touring canoe, but you are not likely to venture out in one of these until you have acquired considerable skill). However, it is as well to be prepared for an emergency so that you can minimize its unfortunate effects.

Don't get flustered, that's the most important thing to remember. Presumably, you will be able to swim, or you would not be venturing out in a canoe at all. So you can only cause damage to yourself or your belongings if you do something rash—as, for example, leaving your canoe to look after itself while you retrieve a drifting paddle. Instead, take a firm hold of one end of the canoe and try to guide it, by pushing or pulling it as you swim towards the bank. Use the current to help you, if you possibly can.

Don't try to right your canoe and climb into it while you are still in deep water, or you will break the air lock inside and admit more water than is in there already. All the water will have to be removed before you can become canoe-borne again, but draining has to be done very carefully or a dangerous strain may be put upon the framework or the fabric of your craft.

Avoiding accidents. Most canoeing accidents can be avoided by the use of a little common sense. Here are a few of the rules that all canoeists should try to remember:

All craft give way to sail, so keep well away from all yachts and sailing dinghies.

Give way to large power-driven craft, too. Their navigators may not find it quite as easy to alter course as you can!

If you find yourself approaching another boat rather rapidly, so that there is likely to be a head-on crash, alter course at once to starboard (that is, to your right hand). The other boat—if its navigator has been well trained—will alter course to starboard too, and a collision will be avoided.

Weirs. Don't take any risks with weirs. It may not seem particularly dangerous to shoot a small weir, in fact it will probably seem rather fun, but remember that the water below it may contain all kinds of hidden hazards, such as sharp rocks, splintered timbers, or even pieces of motor frame. There is no disgrace in taking an easier and safer route, even if you have to carry or 'portage' your canoe downstream.

Slalom. This is a canoeing contest in which a number of specially prepared obstacles have to be negotiated in a given length of broken water. Competitors aim to complete the course in as short a time as possible, penalties being enforced by the judges when any of the obstacles are touched or missed out. Definitely a sport to enjoy when you have become a really skilful canoeist!

Further reading

PERCY W. BLANDFORD, *Tackle Canoeing This Way* (Stanley Paul).
WILLIAM G. LUSCOMBE & L. J. BIRD, *Canoeing* (A. & C. Black).
ALEC R. ELLIS AND C. G. BREAMS, *How to Build and Manage a Canoe* (Brown, Son & Ferguson).

Climbing and pot-holing

There are not many hobbies that can be truly said to appeal to our sense of adventure, but climbing and pot-holing are among the most arduous spare-time activities we can take up, to add an extra zest to our leisure hours. They can be dangerous, too, but accidents usually happen to the inexperienced, the tired and the foolhardy and only rarely to those who are fit, properly clad, and reasonably cautious.

Obviously, you can't hope to learn how to scale the north face of the Eiger properly by studying the pages of a book, but here are a few facts that may help you if you have never done any climbing or pot-holing before, and would like to know how exhilarating it is to travel naturally among the highest and lowest places of the earth.

Adventure schools. These are run by a number of competent authorities, and undoubtedly offer the best possible introduction to climbing (and to sailing, canoeing, caving and other outdoor activities, in many cases). The best known courses are, perhaps, those run by the Outward Bound Trust, of 123 Victoria Street, London, SW1, which have as their aim 'Character Training through Adventure'. For information about other courses, write to:

The Central Council of Physical Recreation,
    6 Bedford Square, London, WC2.
The Scottish Council of Physical Recreation,
    4 Queensferry Street, Edinburgh.
The Ogwen Cottage Mountain School,
    Bethesda, Bangor, North Wales.
The Plas Gwynant Adventure School,
    Nant Gwynant, Caernarvonshire, North Wales.
The Mountain Training Centre,
    Fox House Corner, Hathersage Road, Near Sheffield, Yorkshire.
The Lakeland Mountaineering School,
    The Boathouse, Clappersgate, Ambleside, Westmorland.

Courses in rock climbing and mountain craft are also organized by the Youth Hostels Association (Trevelyan House, St Albans, Herts), the Scottish Youth Hostels Association (7 Bruntsfield Crescent, Edinburgh, 10), the Young Men's Christian Association (National Training Centre, Lakeside, Ulverston, Lancs.), and the Mountaineering Association (102A Westbourne Grove, London, W2). The charges made for accommodation and tuition vary, but a holiday spent on one of these courses can be guaranteed to offer excellent value, wherever it is taken.

Clubs. When you have had a certain amount of experience, you will probably want to join a climbing club, where you can meet other enthusiasts, and enjoy the club's facilities, which may include the use of climbing huts, up-to-date equipment, and special travel arrangements. Your local club may or may not welcome novices. To find out, write to:

The Hon. Secretary,
The British Mountaineering Council,
c/o The Alpine Club, 74 South Audley Street, London, W1,

who will put you in touch with the appropriate organization.

Climbing procedure. If you join a beginners' course, you will probably be shown how to read a map, and how to plan a journey in mountainous country, so that you can keep to ridges or sky-lines when you need to, so that you can keep to easy slopes, and so that you can find and follow mountain tracks.

Then, you may be taught the elementary principles of rock climbing on a miniature and easily accessible rock face—possibly, an outcrop. You will be shown all the essential handholds and footholds, how to use climbing ropes so that the dangers of a fall are minimized, how to 'abseil', or slide down on a double rope, and how to make a safe belay. When your instructors are sure that you have mastered these techniques, you will be taken on a series of climbs that become progressively more difficult as you gain experience. Usually, a climb is classified under one of these grades:

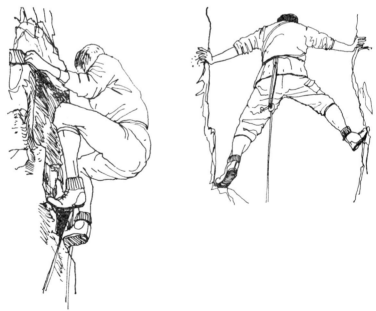

Left A difficult pitch *Right* Climbing a chimney

Easy: With large footholds. Suitable for beginners.
Moderate: Not much more difficult, but having one or two places that are a bit 'sticky'.
Difficult: Usually steeper and more exposed than the first two grades. However, there will be adequate footholds and handholds, which there may not be in a climb that is rated
Very difficult or severe: Eventually, you may graduate to the climbs that have been assessed as 'VERY SEVERE', 'EXTREMELY SEVERE' and 'EXCESSIVELY SEVERE'. These will take you up rock faces that are practically vertical throughout their height, and may even be made more hazardous by occasional overhangs. By that time, you will probably be thinking in terms of the Alps and Everest.

Pot-holing. A pot-hole is a cave that has been formed or eroded so that it is vertical, or nearly so. It is exciting and difficult enough to go exploring a horizontal cave—a pot-hole that can only be safely negotiated by a team of experienced people, with nylon ropes, wire ladders, pulleys, inflatable dinghies, helmets, headlamps and other expensive items of equipment may be a considerable hazard, and quite beyond the resources of the young adventurer. However, the difficulties need not be prohibitive. If you want to see the beauties of the great underground systems in the Mendips, the Peak District, the Yorkshire Dales, South Wales and other limestone districts, you can join one of the well-organized clubs operating in, and within easy reach of those areas. For information write to:

The Hon. Secretary, Mr A. W. Ashwell,
The Cave Research Group of Great Britain,
Cuilcagh, Stanyeld Road, Church Stretton, Shropshire.

Pot-holing is definitely not a hobby for the solitary amateur, and should not be attempted in the same lighthearted way as a country walk.

Further reading
ANTHONY GREENBANK, *Instructions In Rock Climbing* (Museum Press).
SHOWELL STYLES, *How Underground Britain is Explored* (Routledge and Kegan Paul).

Collecting

As soon as they get a chance to spend any length of time in the country or by the seaside, many town dwellers feel the urge to collect and take home some reminders of the happy hours they have enjoyed in the open air. Unfortunately, some people do not collect wisely, and their 'treasures' fade all too quickly or prove a nuisance and have to be thrown away. The week-enders who stream back to London with armfuls of wilting bluebells can get very little pleasure or satisfaction from their rapacity!

But collecting out of doors need not necessarily be a waste of time and energy—if you do a little research it can be one of the most instructive and exciting hobbies of all. Feathers, pebbles, wild flowers, seaweeds, seeds, shells—fine specimens of all these and other natural objects can be sought for, identified (by reference, perhaps, to the books listed below), and suitably displayed. They will make a refreshing change from the subjects such as coins and stamps that more usually appeal to collectors.

Birds' eggs

No book that describes out-of-doors collections would be complete without some mention of birds' eggs, but this is a hobby that has declined in popularity recently as more and more people have come to realize that it is better to enjoy watching birds—with, perhaps, a few discreet glances at their nests—than to destroy their young (which is, after all, what collecting their eggs really amounts to).

Fortunately for our bird population, laws have been passed that reinforce public opinion, and it is now an offence to take the eggs of any birds but a few which have a definite nuisance value. At the time of writing, you may take the eggs of these fifteen birds, as long as you have obtained permission first from the owner of the land on which they are nesting:

Carrion crow	Jay
Cormorant	Magpie
Greater and lesser black-backed gulls	Rook
Herring gull	Shag
Hooded crow	Starling
House sparrow	Stock dove
Jackdaw	Woodpigeon

Scottish naturalists should add three more names to this list—those of the goosander, the red-headed merganser, and the rock dove.

Should you find the eggs of any of these birds, and wish to take one, you will have to remove its contents at the earliest possible moment or that egg will soon be unfit to be included in any collection.

To blow out the white and yoke, make two small holes in the shell, one at each end of the egg, or a single slightly larger hole at the side. Special drills for making these holes can be purchased at any shop that sells equipment for naturalists, or you can use a fine sewing needle or even, if you are far from home, a hawthorn point. Puncture the skin of the yolk as you make one of the holes.

There are two alternative methods once the holes have been made: blowing or sucking—you can put your lips to the shell, or, if you feel a bit squeamish about doing this, you can use a special suction tube or blowpipe. These are obtainable, again, from any naturalists' shop. You will find near the end of the suction tube a bulb in which the contents of the egg will collect. This bulb may have to be washed out two or three times while you are dealing with a very large egg.

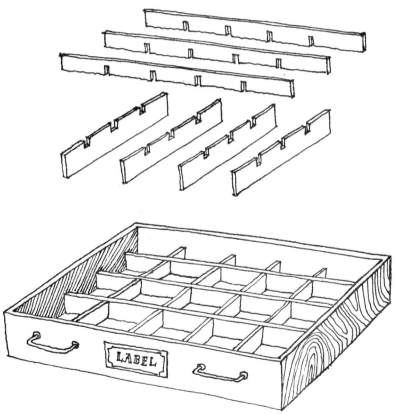

Display and storage cases can be divided quite easily with interlocking strips of plywood or cardboard

It is always advisable to rinse out a newly-blown egg with clean lukewarm water before it is put into store or on display. This should remove the last traces of egg white and leave the shell perfectly wholesome. It is not easy to store birds' eggs safely as they are so very fragile, but you will find it quite simple to divide a drawer, tray or box into small compartments, each of which can contain one egg. One method that can be warmly recommended is shown in the illustration on the previous page.

Feathers

You do not have to be a trained archaeologist or even a dedicated bird-watcher to enjoy collecting feathers. As they are incredibly light, in relation to the work they do, it is not surprising that feathers have only a limited life and eventually have to be replaced. When a bird moults, it is doing this renovation in a wholesale way. Even when it is not moulting, a bird will shed its worn feathers at fairly frequent intervals. That is why there always seem to be feathers around once one starts looking for them.

Unless you happen to see the bird that it actually comes from, you may not be able to identify the original owner of a feather, but you may find that the colour and pattern will give you a clue to the bird's habits and way of life.

Some birds, for instance, are able to carry on their business in an entirely unobtrusive way, as the colour and markings of their plumage help to form a most satisfactory camouflage. A wren in its grey and brown livery may be almost invisible in the dead leaves and grass at the base of a hedge. The woodcock and the partridge with their barred brown and buff feathers may escape detection quite easily in autumnal undergrowth. You will probably come across many other examples.

Sometimes, you may find feathers that are especially beautiful or especially brilliant. These may have been evolved so that a bird shall seem abnormally ferocious (a robin's red breast must surely play a large part in frightening other birds off this fierce little creature's private territory), for recognition purposes, or, at certain seasons, so that the bird may attract a suitable mate. Where male and female birds have different plumage it is often—though not always—the male bird that has the more striking attire.

Keep flat feathers sealed away under cellophane or polythene in a loose-leaf book or album. If you find any feathers that have a pronounced curve, put them in suitable mothproof boxes.

Pebbles

When you go for a walk along a beach in the wake of an ebbing tide you will notice, if you look closely at the rocks, stones and sand around you, certain pebbles that seem to shine out from all the others on account of their colour, or their translucence, or their texture, or that strange indefinable quality we usually call 'charm'.

It is unlikely that you will be lucky enough to find a truly precious and therefore valuable stone when you are away on a seaside holiday, though some very impure sapphires are occasionally found on the Isle of Mull, real aquamarines have been picked up on the Welsh coast, and someone in Suffolk was once fortunate enough to come across a large block of amber worth several thousands of pounds. But that was more than a century ago, and there have been no such sensational finds since then!

The pebbles you do see will provide you with a most interesting and decorative collection, though, on some beaches, you may pick up some really attractive semi-precious stones, such as the light purple or violet *amethystine quartz* (*amethyst*), the lemon yellow or gold *citrine*, the beautifully marked *agate*, the translucent fleshy pink *carnelian*, and the lovely straight-banded *onyx*. Many of these stones are really delightful when they are cut and polished, and they are often made up into brooches and pendants.

Unfortunately, most of the pebbles you pick up will have acquired on their tide-borne travels a thin skin of carbonate of lime or some other obscuring crust. You will not find it easy to cut and polish them yourself, but there are skilled lapidarists at many seaside resorts who will do the job for you, using special steel saws and diamond paste. As they charge for their services, you will only want to take them your most attractive specimens.

To get as much pleasure as possible from pebble-collecting, you should know something about the kind of rock from which each of your treasures has been produced. Take a sharp strong knife with you, so that you can scrape away a little of the disguising outer skin. Take a small hammer, too, so that you can study the texture and structure of any pebble you don't mind 'damaging' by breaking off one end, to produce a freshly fractured surface. (Be very careful how you do this, incidentally—it is only too easy to cause a sharp splinter to fly up into an eye, with disastrous results. A sharp tap should break most pebbles and a cloth over the pebble will keep the fragments from flying up.) Finally, take with you a pocket lens or magnifying glass to make possible a really close study of the surfaces your knife and your hammer have revealed.

If you acquire an elementary knowledge of geology you should be able to allot each of your pebbles, after you have given it a thorough inspection, to one of these three classes:

Igneous: Formed when the earth's crust was in a molten state.
Sedimentary: Formed by the deposition of sands and other particles over a long period of time.
Metamorphic: Changed from its original state by intense heat or tremendous pressure.

Every pebble in your collection, in fact, may give you some clue to part of the earth's history. Once you have learned some of the secrets of stones you will never find a beach walk boring again.

Pressed flowers

From the joyful moments when the last spring snowdrifts are melting away to the first sharp frost of the following winter there is an everchanging succession of wild flowers in our fields, hedgerows and woods, and on our mountainsides.

Some wild flowers such as the daisy and buttercup are so common that we would hardly think them worth a collector's attention. Others, such as the Monkey Orchid (*Orchis Simia*), are so rare that they may

Kingcup

A typical Labiate (deadnettle)

only be found in one or two remote places, and have to be guarded carefully in case they become extinct. Between these two extremes there are scores of beautifully formed and subtly coloured botanical specimens that you can find, garner and preserve. If any one of these is displayed carefully on the page of an album it will be a splendid

74

reminder of the landscape in which you found it, as well as being most pleasant to look at, and to show your friends.

Collecting wild flowers is a hobby that calls for very little equipment. You will need a spoon or a small trowel with which to dig up your specimens, a box or tin with a tight-fitting lid in which you can carry them safely home, and a press. This, the only item that may be at all difficult to acquire, can either be bought ready made or improvised from two drawing boards or some other flat pieces of

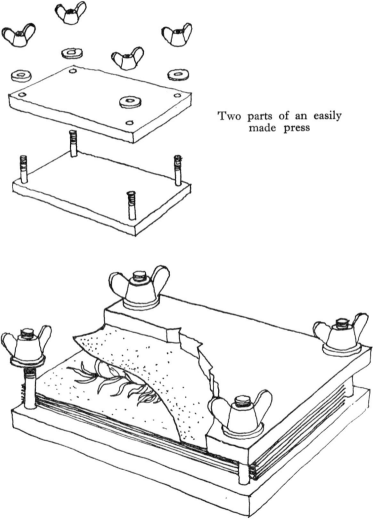

Two parts of an easily
made press

Wild flowers can be pressed in clean blotting paper between two flat smooth pieces of wood

wood. Bolts, washers and wing nuts can be used for clamping these together and exerting the necessary pressure, or, alternatively, they can be placed under some heavy pieces of furniture.

When you find a flower that you would like to include in your collection, choose if you can a specimen that shows every stage of its development from the first appearance of the buds to the final formation of the seed pods. You may have to return several times to a site before you find a plant that is exactly right.

As soon as you get your specimens home, put them in your press before they have had a chance to wilt. Put two or three sheets of clean blotting paper in first, and then arrange one of your specimens on the upper surface of the top sheet. Don't just throw the plant down and leave it—try to arrange the stem, leaves, buds and flowers so that they will be composed, when they are pressed, dried and fixed, in a convincingly natural way. When you are satisfied, put two or three more sheets of blotting paper over the plant and then, if you wish, another specimen. You can deal with quite a large number of plants in a press at one and the same time as long as each is separated from the next by a layer of absorbent paper. To get really good results, you should change the paper every two or three days until you are sure that all the moisture has been extracted from the plant (it is impossible to say how long this will take—a plant with a thick woody stem and pulpy leaves will obviously need a longer time in the press than a delicate plant such as a harebell).

When the pressed specimens are ready for mounting, arrange each of them carefully on a rectangular piece of card or mounting board and fix it in position with a few narrow strips of Sellotape. You can use gummed paper instead, but this is a little more noticeable. Add a label, on which you have written the name of the plant, where you found it, and any other details you think may be useful for record purposes. Then cover the sheet with a piece of cellophane, to keep out dust.

Seaweeds

Seaweed collecting may seem a strange and unfashionable hobby, but if you live or are spending a holiday near a rocky stretch of coast you can find specimens that may have considerable scientific interest, as well as being extremely decorative.

Approximately eight hundred different marine 'algae' are said to have been found in British waters alone, but you will be extremely fortunate if you can add even half as many as that to your collection, however thoroughly you search, since many varieties are so tiny that they cannot possibly be identified without the aid of a microscope.

Most seaweeds spend their early life in one fixed position—anchored, possibly, to a rock, a groyne, a large shell, or even to some other seaweed. They do not need the same kind of widely spread roots as a land plant since they are surrounded on all sides by the water that nourishes them. Instead, they have to produce some other tenacious gripper that will keep them from being torn away by powerful currents. This anchor is usually known as a 'holdfast'.

You will not need much equipment for collecting seaweeds. You will find useful:

A plastic bag or plastic bucket, so that you can keep your specimens in salt water until you are ready to dry and mount them
A large dish
Some butter muslin
Blotting paper

And, for the mounts, some suitable sheets of strong, unglazed paper or thin card.

First, put a sheet of the mounting paper in the dish, and cover it to a depth of at least one-half an inch with salt water. (Don't try to use fresh water, or you will probably find that the seaweed will change colour.)

Put into the dish one of the pieces of seaweed you wish to mount, easing the various parts of it out so that it seems to be floating quite naturally, and in a pleasantly decorative way.

Then lift the paper gently out of the water so that the seaweed is raised with it, and the water drains away.

Put the wet paper on to a sheet of blotting paper or some other absorbent surface and cover it with one thickness of butter muslin. You can add further mounts, with their specimens, to the pile as long as you protect each with a piece of butter muslin in the same way. Don't try to apply any pressure, though, or you will crush the tender seaweeds and make them quite valueless as items for your collection. During the next few days, change the blotting paper three or four times and you will find at the end of that time that all the unwanted moisture will have been extracted and that the dried seaweeds will have glued themselves to their mounts by their own natural mucilage. If any fronds should become detached when you pull the butter muslin away you can use some tiny strips of Sellotape to fasten them back in place.

Seeds

It is quite easy to go to a shop and buy a packet of seeds. It is easy, too, to sow those seeds under the correct conditions in the soil of your garden. By carrying out these two simple actions you will be doing one of Nature's most difficult jobs for her.

If you want a really unusual subject for a collection, you can have a most interesting time looking for and finding seeds that have been dispersed by trees and plants without human aid. You should be able to deduce, from the structure of the seeds, how each would be propelled.

First, there are the seeds that are carried by movements of air. You will probably have watched the fairy-like seed carriers of the thistle and the dandelion as they stream past on the wind; you may have had fun with the whirling, propellor-like seeds released by the sycamore; but do you know the more intricate 'flying machines' of the lime tree, or the little light discs thrown off by the elm? The pine, the ash and the hornbeam also produce seeds that fall (or glide) into this category.

Then there are the seeds that rely on animals for transport. These usually hook themselves on to the hairs and fleeces of passing beasts —and, if we get near enough to the plant that is trying to lose them, on to our clothes too. The burdock, goosegrass, hound's-tongue and enchanter's nightshade are fairly common examples of plants whose seeds are generally animal-borne.

Lastly, there are the seeds that are dispersed by a minor explosion —by the sudden bursting of a seedpod as it ripens in the sun, or by

Grass seeds are largely wind carried

the splitting and twisting of a dried-up husk. The laburnum, the vetch and the broom all get rid of their seeds in this way—if you sit by any gorse bushes on a hot summer's day listen carefully and you may actually be able to hear the seeds being 'fired'!

So, keep on the look-out for seeds and seedlings when you are out of doors in the country and try to discover how they have reached the spot in which you have found them.

Shells

Have you ever held a shell up to your ear and heard the sound of the wild sea waves breaking on a beach? Have you ever asked yourself how many different kinds of seashell you could see on one particular stretch of shore? If the answer to either of those questions is 'yes', you will probably agree that a collection of shells may be one of the best souvenirs you can bring back from a seaside holiday.

Shells are light, easy to store and display, and, being formed chiefly of carbonate of lime, are in virtually no danger of decay. Several hundred marine molluscs have been identified in British waters alone, most of them bearing shells that are extremely beautiful. Some of the greatest modern sculptors, who prize perfection of shape above all other natural qualities, have found inspiration in the curved and tapering forms of shells, and painters have revelled in their subtle and evocative colourings.

Before you have been collecting shells for long, you will probably realize that all your specimens are falling into two distinct classes: there will be the single shells (usually spiral) of the *univalves*, of which good examples are the limpets, the whelks and the snails; and there will be the shells of the *bivalves*, that are made up, as their name implies, of two halves or 'valves'. Among the molluscs that can be allotted to the latter class are the clams, the oysters, the cockles and the mussels. Later, you will probably want to classify your specimens more exactly, and then you will need one of the books listed at the end of this chapter.

Signs

'DANGER: MEN AT WORK', 'CAUTION: RACEHORSES CROSS HERE',
'WARNING: STEEP HILL WITH BENDS' . . . You will see signs as dramatic
as these wherever public highways have been constructed. You can
get a lot of amusement from recording any unusual examples you
may come across, either by photographing them or by sketching
them or (if this suits you better) by writing verbal descriptions of
them. Sign collecting may be a most useful way of relieving the
tedium on a very long journey.

Roadside messages and traffic warnings are not the only noteworthy signs you can record for your collection. National Parks,
Forestry Commission plantations and Nature Reserves are well provided with signs, and so are the tracts of land used by the armed
forces. Occasionally you may come across a sign that has been
carved out of a block of wood or stone by some local craftsman, or
a sign made of wrought iron, or a sign so large that it stretches right
over a road. These are the rarities that keen sign-collectors look out
for, and tell each other about, when they compare notes at the end
of their holidays.

For many centuries, tradesmen of various kinds have had their
own easily recognizable signs—the barber's pole and the pawn-
broker's golden globes are well-known examples—and these are well
worth looking for. So, too, are the small embossed metal plaques
you may see on some old buildings that were placed there by the
original fire insurance companies. Only premises that bore the mark
were eligible for the attentions of that company's firefighters in case
of emergency! If, on looking round, you see signs of so many
different kinds that the prospect of recording them seems daunting,
you may well decide to specialize. You can get plenty of fun, for
instance, if you concentrate on inn signs. 'The Crooked Billet', 'The
Lamb and Packet', and 'The Hanging Gate' are found in several
districts, and it is quite easy to discover how these places of refreshment got their names. But what do you think were the origins of
'The Blade Bone', 'The Merry Month' and 'The Woodin's Shades'?
Once you start collecting signs you will find yourself trying to solve
all kinds of intriguing mysteries.

Skeleton leaves

Occasionally, you will find in the base of a hedge or in some other undisturbed spot a dead leaf from which all the soft fleshy matter has been removed by the slow processes of the weather, leaving only the harder 'leaf skeleton' with its fantastically delicate tracery.

You will probably enjoy collecting skeleton leaves, but you are not likely to find it a particularly exciting hobby unless you take some steps to increase the supply of available specimens. Fortunately, it is not only possible to turn a green leaf into a most beautiful skeleton in a matter of hours, but you can have a lot of fun in the process. For your de-fleshing vat you will need a saucepan that is half or three-quarters full of water (no more), and a little washing soda. If you allow one dessertspoonful of soda to each pint of water you will produce a solution that is strong enough to deal with all but the very toughest leaves. On no account should the solution be any stronger than this, and do be careful not to let it touch your skin, or to splash up in or near your eyes, or the results may be painful, or worse. Heat the solution up slowly, until it is a few degrees below boiling point. Then put your leaf into the hot fluid and let it float around for a little more than an hour. Keep a lid on the pan while the liquid is simmering.

When the time is up, take the leaf out of the solution and try to worry the softened flesh away with a stiff-bristled brush. If the flesh does not seem to want to come away, put the leaf back in the pan and let it simmer there for a few more minutes.

When you have finally succeeded in reducing the leaf to its skeleton tracery, you will have to wash every vestige of soda away or the skeleton will soon vanish, too. Put it in a dish or bowl and let the water from a cold tap run gently over it for an hour or so. At the end of that time it should be safe from further corrosive action.

Then put the skeleton on a piece of clean blotting paper and mount it, when it is dry, on a suitable piece of thick paper or card. A dark background will display the lace-like quality of the veins to their best advantage.

Walking sticks

Most of the things that you collect will be both decorative and interesting, but not many may be useful as well! Walking sticks and staffs are splendid things to own if you are fond of rambling, and as they do not need much storage room you will not inconvenience anybody if you decide to form quite a large collection.

81

Like many objects associated with more leisurely days, walking sticks are now distinctly 'out of fashion', and this is fortunate for the collector, for there are few junk-shops that do not contain at least one bundle of old walking sticks that are being practically given away. The best specimens to look for are, of course, the sticks with some distinctive quality, such as the sticks with beautifully carved or whittled handles or stems, sticks made from unusually attractive woods, and sticks with some special associations (as, for example, sticks that have belonged to famous men, or that have been made from the branches of trees with some historical interest). You may even be able to find a genuine sword-stick for your collection, but if you do, don't leave it about where any young children or irresponsible persons can find it, or the results may be unfortunate!

Further reading

General
GUY R. WILLIAMS, *Instructions to Young Collectors* (Museum Press).

Pebbles
CLARENCE ELLIS, *The Pebbles on the Beach* (Faber and Faber).

Pressed Flowers
EDWARD STEP, *Wayside and Woodland Blossoms* (Frederick Warne).
PATRICIA LEWIS, *British Wild Flowers* (Eyre and Spottiswoode).

Seaweeds
CAROLA I. DICKINSON, *British Seaweeds* (Eyre and Spottiswoode).

Seeds
MILLICENT E. SELSAM, *Things to do with Seeds* (Chatto and Windus).

Shells
PHILIP STREET, *Shell Life on the Seashore* (Faber and Faber).

Cycling

There are many different ways of getting yourself from Place A to Place B, and you may have discovered already that cycling is one of the most enjoyable, especially on quiet roads and with companions who appreciate a journey made in a comparatively leisurely fashion. Of course, if you have ambitions to be a successful competitor in time trials or road or track races, or if you want to exhaust yourself in the vigorous activity known as 'cyclo cross' you will chafe at the very idea of such a slow pace, but that only pinpoints one of the enormous advantages of bicycles—they can be used for such a wide variety of purposes.

Choosing a bicycle. There are very few bad bicycles on the market nowadays, but even a high-quality expensive bicycle will give you little pleasure if it does not suit your requirements exactly. Here are some of the things you ought to think about before you make a final decision:

Weight. Every extra ounce your bicycle weighs will take an extra amount of your energy when you are trying to move it—and this will seem especially important when you are riding uphill or on the level against a headwind. Most of the best modern bicycles have frames made from Reynold's '531' high tensile steel tubing, and are much stronger and lighter than bicycles made of ordinary steels. Special light alloy fittings are incorporated, too, to help cut down the total load.

Workmanship. There is no point in pedalling away furiously if the energy you are expending is not harnessed with the maximum efficiency. All the bearings in a bicycle must be in perfect condition, properly adjusted and well lubricated if friction is not to act as a constant brake that you could very well do without. Don't be satisfied unless you have a chance to test thoroughly the action of any bicycle you are offered.

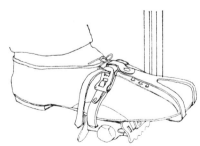

Foot attachment for racing cyclist

Rigidity. This, too, is important, since a bicycle with a frame that is not properly rigid will quickly tire the rider.

Comfort. Don't be persuaded to buy any bicycle that is not completely comfortable, or be swayed in your judgement by its superficial appearance or the 'sportiness' of the fittings. You should be able to take up a good riding position, with your weight distributed evenly over both wheels, and you should be able to stay in that position for most of a day without feeling any strain. A bicycle that does not allow you to put both feet on the ground without raising yourself off your saddle will be too large for you.

Among the accessories you may find useful are these:

A saddlebag. For carrying food, waterproof clothing, maps, and any other extras such as a camera or a pair of binoculars you may need on your journey a spacious canvas saddlebag can hardly be bettered. Light metal frames can be obtained that fit on the back of the saddle and keep the weight of the saddlebag from bearing on the mudguard.

When extra luggage has to be taken—as, for example, when you are setting out on a cycling holiday—you can add a handlebar bag and/or a pair of panniers. Some people like to wear rucksacks when they are cycling, but it is less tiring to have the back and shoulders free.

A water bottle. Your cycle will probably take you to all kinds of lonely places where ice creams and cups of tea are not immediately available. You will be glad, then, if you are carrying some light refreshment with you. Special bottles can be obtained, with holders that are fixed on to the handlebars or some other part of the frame. These bottles can be used to hold water, soft drinks or natural fruit juices, according to your taste.

Tools. Obviously, you won't want to go far without a few tools at least to enable you to repair punctures and deal with other small mishaps, but equally obviously you won't want to carry too many because of their weight. Normally, you can 'get by' with a standard puncture repair outfit, three tyre levers and an adjustable spanner, but when you are going touring in any remote country districts where it may be difficult to get help you can also include some, if not all, of these:

A screwdriver
A 'C' spanner (use in inaccessible places where adjustable spanners are not well suited)
A peg-and-cone spanner (use where extra pressure is needed)
A chain rivet remover
A cotter pin remover
A spare inner tube
And spare chain links, hub nuts, and bulbs
for your lighting system.

84

Clothing. In fine weather you can wear almost any clothes in which you will feel comfortable and which will allow you to move your limbs freely. Clothes which are too loose or too floppy are generally inconvenient, especially in windy weather. Double-seated shorts, for summer, and plus-four type garments for winter are favoured by most experienced touring cyclists, and so are the specially designed windproof jackets stocked by most cycle dealers.

Cycling in wet weather can be really uncomfortable unless you are properly equipped. Waterproof capes are found most generally suitable, as they allow freedom of movement (when they are sufficiently large) and can be packed away into a very small space when the weather improves. Most capes have loops for the wrists or thumbs, and some have fastening tapes for the waist, too. It is advisable to use these fittings, as a flapping cape can be a nuisance, and sometimes dangerous.

A sou'wester will keep your head dry when you are cycling in wet weather, but some people prefer berets and others prefer caps. Cloth headwear may take rather a long time to dry if it gets soaked.

Shoes used for cycling should be light and fairly flexible, so that the foot and the pedal will work well together. You will not need shoe-plates unless you are going in seriously for cycle racing.

Setting out. Before you set out, you should see that the handlebars and saddle of your bicycle are properly adjusted, so that your body and legs will be in an efficient and comfortable position.

Sitting up straight in the saddle like a begging dog will slow you up: crouching low over the handlebars will prevent you seeing much of the countryside you are passing through, and may give you cramp: a compromise, whereby your body leans forward at approximately 45°, can be relied upon to make the best possible use of all your muscles and will distribute your weight equally over the two wheels so that you can steer without wobbling.

Check both brakes, too, before you leave home, in case they require readjustment. It is easy to form this habit—and it can be dangerous if you forget.

Maintenance. A clean and well-maintained bicycle seems wonderfully easy to ride. It is better to spend a few minutes at fairly frequent intervals on servicing your machine than to neglect it for months until it needs a complete and time-consuming overhaul.

Chief among the routine jobs you should remember are these:

Check and adjust the brakes (already mentioned).
Check the wheel bearings.
Tighten the nuts on the pedals, if they have worked loose.
Test the chain for wear and tighten it if it has become slack.
Treat the saddle with leather soap or one of the preparations sold specially by cycle dealers.

Oil all parts that need lubrication.

Replace any part of your lighting equipment that could possibly fail before the next servicing.

None of these tasks is very difficult to carry out. You will find clear and comprehensive instructions in an excellent book *The Cycle Book of Maintenance*, published by the Temple Press.

Punctures. If you have a good pump, a repair outfit, and three tyre levers a flat tyre should not worry you unduly.

First, check that the air has not escaped through a fault in the valve. To do this, you will have to remove the valve nut to examine the valve rubber or insert. If the valve seems to be working properly, try to locate the puncture. Sometimes you can do this by listening for the sound of escaping air. If that fails, you may have to pull the inner tube from under the tyre cover so that you can try immersion in water. (When you are going on a long journey, you may find it advisable to take a spare inner tube with you, so that you can repair a puncture at a convenient time and place. When replacing an inner tube, you will have to remove the wheel temporarily from the bicycle, but this is not difficult with a modern bicycle. If the bicycle has roller lever brakes, you may have to remove one of the shoes.)

Some people find it hard to remove the outer cover of a tyre from the rim of the wheel to get access to the inner tube. This is the easiest procedure:

First, unscrew the lock-nut that is holding the valve stem firmly in position.

Then use the end of one of your tyre levers to raise the edge of the outer cover over the rim of the wheel. Do this very carefully. If you pinch the inner tube with the end of the lever you may cause a worse puncture than the one you are trying to repair (it is sometimes possible to push an inner tube out of harm's way with the end of one finger).

Insert the end of a second lever under the cover an inch or two away from the first. You will notice a small notch in one side of each lever. This will enable you to anchor that lever back on to a spoke of the wheel while it is in use.

Then work outwards, raising the cover over the rim of the wheel a little at a time until it shows no tendency to spring back. After that, you will find it quite easy to pull the rest of the cover over the rim of the wheel with your fingers alone.

When you have located a puncture, dry the area round the hole, clean it with the fine glasspaper you will find in your repair outfit, and choose a patch that will give it adequate cover.

Then take the rubber adhesive supplied in the outfit and apply a thin coat over the whole area that the patch is to occupy. Let this dry, and then add a second coat. Before the second coat has had a chance to dry, take the protective cover from the repair patch and press it down firmly over the puncture. Keep up this pressure for a minute or two, then dab a little french chalk (this also will be included in the repair outfit) over the whole area. Make sure that there are no thorns or sharp splinters of any kind still in the tyre cover, then replace the inner tube.

Begin by passing the valve stem through the hole in the rim. Then see that the inner tube is lying satisfactorily under the cover, without any twists. Then start to lift the cover back over the rim of the wheel, starting at a point immediately opposite the valve. If the inner tube shows any tendency to become trapped, pump a very little air into the tube.

Clubs. There are many advantages in joining a cyclists' club or association: you will get advice and information, you will be able to go on well-organized runs, and you will meet people who have the interests of all cyclists at heart. But do choose a club that caters for *your* requirements—some clubs are intended for racing cyclists only, and will have little appeal for the ordinary tourist.

The Cyclists' Tourist Association (Headquarters: 3 Craven Hill, London, W2) is the largest and most influential body. Members can get advice about routes and foreign travel, free insurance against third party risks, and free legal advice and aid.

The British Cycling Federation (Headquarters: 21 Blackfriars Road, London, SE1) also offers advice and insurance facilities, but caters more especially for sporting and racing cyclists.

The Highway Code. All cyclists should study the Highway Code and remember all the standards of conduct laid down there that can possibly affect them. Cyclists are among the most vulnerable of road-users, but many accidents can be avoided by the use of a little courtesy and commonsense.

The law and cyclists. All cyclists have to obey certain laws designed for their own safety, and that of the other people on the road. At the time of writing, these are the most important points to remember:

Brakes. Any bicycle which has wheels exceeding 18 in. in diameter must have two efficient brakes, one on each wheel and they must act independently of each other. Bicycles with wheel diameters of 18 in. or less must have one efficient brake. A bicycle with a 'fixed' wheel is considered to have a brake on the rear wheel, and needs to have only one other brake, which must act on the front wheel.

Lights. Check that the lights on your bicycle conform to the necessary British Standard Specifications. You will need a white front light, a red rear light, and a red rear reflector before you can go out legally after lighting up time. Lights have to be fixed in a standard position, too (the rear light must not be less than 15 in. and not more than 3 ft. 6 in. from the ground, and it must not be more than 20 in. from the extreme rear of the machine). If your lights fail, don't try to be clever and ride on in the dark. Dismount, and wheel your machine carefully home.

Further reading

RONALD ENGLISH, *Cycling for You* (Lutterworth Press).
A. L. PULLEN, *The Cycling Handbook* (Pitman).
KENNETH BOWDEN, *Cycle Racing* (Temple Press).
C. R. WOODWARD, *Scientific Training for Cycling* (Temple Press).

Fossil hunting

Fossils are the remains of animals or plants that have been preserved in rocks through tens and perhaps hundreds of centuries. The study of fossils is a very important branch of geology because through these extraordinary discoveries we can trace the history of much of the earth's surface and of the fascinating creatures that have lived on it through the ages. It is not a hobby that can be recommended as a pastime for just one or two afternoons, but if you are patient and have an enquiring mind you may find that 'palaeontology' (to give its proper and rather impressive name) is one of the most engrossing outdoor activities of all.

The first man to discover how each stratum or layer of rock could be scientifically related to other layers by the organic remains it contained was the famous William Smith (1769–1839) who has been rightly called the 'Father of English Geology'. Although he was born and brought up in a remote Oxfordshire village and had a comparatively crude education, Smith was able to prepare and publish in 1815 the first geological map for England, Wales and Southern Scotland.

When the importance of his researches was realized, the Geological Survey of Great Britain was set up with a staff of officers to carry out more extensive investigations and to make detailed geological maps available to the general public. As you will only find fossil-hunting a fully rewarding hobby if you understand the geological structure of the area you are studying, you may decide to invest in one of these. Unfortunately, all unsold copies of the Old Series, together with the plates from which they were printed, were destroyed when Southampton was bombed during the Second World War. New maps are now appearing as the areas are re-surveyed and can be obtained from Edward Stanford Ltd, 12 Long Acre, London, WC2,

or through any large bookseller. If you have any difficulty, or if you want some really local information, you can consult the officials at your nearest museum.

How to find fossils. Nearly all fossils are found in sedimentary rocks—that is, in rocks formed by the slow deposition of solid matter, which was afterwards compressed by the deposition of further layers.

It is a waste of time looking for them in 'metamorphic' rocks, for they would never have survived the extraordinary pressures and the high temperatures in which those rocks took their final form. It is useless, too, to look for them in igneous rocks of the 'plutonic' kind, for these originated far away below the earth's crust, where no life existed at all. A few fossils are found in rocks formed of volcanic ash, but these must have got into the ash after it cooled, and before it was compressed sufficiently to become an impenetrable rock.

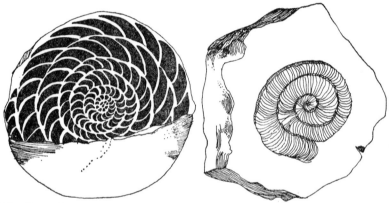

Nautilus—the creature builds further chambers as it grows

The sedimentary rocks you will find richest in fossils are chalk, limestone and shale. These were all formed under water by a process that lasted for many centuries, and the fossils you will find in them are most likely to be those of marine organisms. You can dig fossils out of a limestone or shale cliff quite easily with a hammer and chisel, while chalk is so soft that fossils may be extracted from it without any difficulty with a pocket knife.

Not all the fossils you find will be the actual remnants of animals or plants that lived a very long time ago. Frequently, the buried organism would decay, leaving in the rock a depression or hole that was an exact replica of itself. Over the centuries silica, carbonate of lime or some other soluble material would be washed down into this hole, which would act as a mould. Gradually the mould would be filled up, until the creature that had formed it would be exactly reproduced in a material that was—and is—itself as hard as stone.

Fossils to look for. Among the fossils you may enjoy looking out for are these:

Graptolites. These are little marine organisms that led a very restricted form of existence many millions of years ago. They looked rather like thin horny rods—sometimes straight, sometimes forked, and sometimes branching. You can find graptolite fossils in the dark shales of Wales and Scotland. You will recognize them if you remember that they may resemble small pieces of fretsaw blade.

Tribolites. These little creatures have also been extinct for hundreds of millions of years. Normally they would wander about on the sea floor looking for food, and they were the forerunners of the 'crustaceans' we know so well today—lobsters, crabs, crayfish and prawns. You may find tribolite fossils in limestone and shale, and you will recognize them if you remember that they looked rather like large woodlice, with bodies clothed in thin, segmented armour.

Brachiopods. These were bivalves, with beautifully formed symmetrical shells. Limestones and shales may contain large numbers of brachiopod fossils, which are always worth collecting.

Ammonites. These were creatures that produced and lived in, spirally covered shells that resembled rams' horns. That was how they got their name—Ammon was an Egyptian deity with a horned head. Occasionally, you may hear them called 'snakestones', for there is a legend that snakes once became so numerous at Whitby, on the Yorkshire coast, that the Abbess of Whitby had to lay a curse on them. The curse was so powerful that the snakes lost their heads and curled up and died! Look for ammonite fossils in chalk, limestone and shale. They are to be found in great profusion (as you might expect) near Whitby.

If you are prepared to do the necessary research, there is no reason why you should not become quite adept at finding and identifying these and many other interesting fossils. You may never attain quite as much fame as Mary Anning, of Lyme Regis, who discovered an almost complete skeleton of a Plesiosaurus, but then the fossils of extinct aquatic reptiles that were nearly six feet long are not come across very often!

Further reading
H. H. Swinnerton, *Fossils* (Collins).
Kai Petersen, *Prehistoric Life on Earth* (Methuen).
Robin Place, *Finding Fossil Man* (Rockcliff).

Gardening

'A garden,' the poet tells us, 'is a lovesome thing'.

Your plot of ground may already be exactly that, with smooth green lawns, ornamental trees, flower beds that are a riot of colour, and a few less conventional features, such as an Alpine slope and a herbarium, for extra pleasure.

You may, on the other hand, be just starting to garden, or just about to start with a small square of uncultivated earth, a back yard, or just an unfilled tub as your only territorial advantage.

Whichever is the case, you will already have experienced the compulsive urge to grow beautiful plants of your own choice, in your own way, that besets so many people who enjoy spending their time out of doors. Gardening is more than a hobby—it is almost a mania!

Equipment. Unfortunately, no garden will flourish and be a joy to look at, and to be in, unless a certain amount of work has been done to prepare the soil, to establish the plants, and to remove any undesirable weeds. The jobs are not exactly endless, but they have a habit of cropping up at closely repeated intervals. Luckily for us, equipment is now available that makes even the heaviest gardening jobs comparatively enjoyable.

For large gardens, motor mowers and mechanical cultivators have been designed that remove most of the back-breaking toil from lawn-cutting and bed-digging. It is difficult to do without these if you have large areas of grass or soil to keep in good fettle, but for small gardens you will need (beside a lawn mower) only:

A spade
A garden fork
A hand fork
A Dutch hoe
A rake
Shears (if there are hedges to trim)
A pruning knife (or pair of secateurs)

and some means of watering your plants—a hose with a sprinkler, if you have made the necessary arrangements with your Water Board, or a watering can.

Don't let any shortage of equipment stop you from gardening—an enthusiast will make a barren plot produce a profusion of flowers with no implements more ambitious than a tablespoon and fork, and a pair of scissors. A plastic bucket will do for a small garden what a wheelbarrow does for a large garden.

Planning. Even the smallest garden or window box needs careful planning if it is to give you as much pleasure as possible. Here are a few things to bear in mind:

The suitability of your soil. It is a mistake to think that all kinds of plant will do equally well in any one particular type of soil. Some plants, such as roses, prefer clay; others, such as azaleas and rhododendrons, cannot stand an acid soil. Somewhere in your district there will be some knowledgeable person—a nurseryman, perhaps, or the local government officer responsible for parks and gardens—who will look at a sample of your soil and give you on-the-spot advice.

Plant for the seasons. Without a large outlay you can have flowers in your garden during nine months at least of every year. Read a nurseryman's catalogue carefully, and you will be able to make a list of plants that will be successively colourful, from the scillas and crocuses in very early spring to the Michaelmas daisies and red-hot pokers in late autumn.

Transplanting a seedling

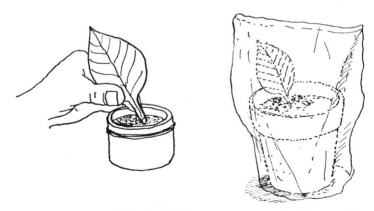

Cuttings can be successful with the help of a transparent plastic bag to keep in moisture

Plant for height. As a general rule, it is a good idea to follow the old precept 'shortest at the front, tallest at the back'. So, flowers can be banked from the tiny alyssum, as a border, to hollyhocks and climbing roses as a magnificent backcloth.

Hardy annuals. Any duffer can get a wonderful display of summer flowers by investing a few shillings in the seeds of hardy annuals. The seedlings are tough enough to withstand any late frosts that may be left over from winter, the flowers are usually highly colourful, and the spent plants can be cleared away when the summer is over without leaving any ugly gaps.

Excellent hardy annuals with which you can gain valuable gardening experience are the cornflowers (traditionally blue, but also obtainable in white and pink); larkspurs (purples and blues); godetia (red to pale pink); the pale blue nigella, or Love in a Mist, with its delicate foliage; Shirley poppies (white and pink); stocks, of various kinds such as 'Ten Week' and 'Night-scented'; and the bold nasturtiums, which range from lemon yellow, through orange, flame, vermilion and scarlet to deep crimson.

This is how you can get the best results with hardy annuals:

First, give the ground a light dusting with a proprietary fertilizer, and then break up the soil so that there are no large lumps in it.

Then drag a stick or the back of a rake across the area you have chosen for the seeds so that a number of shallow, narrow furrows are formed. Sow the seeds thinly in these furrows, then rake the soil gently over them and pat the surface lightly with the flat of a spade.

Left The leaves of the popular Pelargonium (geranium) often have an exciting smell *Right* Plants can be increased by gently separating roots and replanting

94

After that, don't swamp the ground with water, but give a gentle sprinkle if the soil becomes very dry. When the seedlings appear, thin out the weaker ones to avoid overcrowding, pick off any slugs that may appear, and then wait to enjoy the results of your efforts!

Perennials. Perennials that are easy for the amateur to grow are numerous, and you will be able to get some tempting ideas by studying any good nurseryman's catalogue. Among the well-tried favourites are:

Lupins. Russell lupins can introduce masses of subtle colours into your flower beds in midsummer.

Delphiniums. These send up lovely pale blue, rich blue and mauve spires in June and July.

Pinks. Short, sweetly scented, and splendid for the front edges of a flowerbed. They are not fussy about soil, and can be easily propagated. Just take cuttings or pipings (that is, cuttings pulled out at a joint instead of being cut) and insert them in sandy soil in a frame or sheltered border outdoors in June or July.

Marigolds. Useful for the late summer garden, with their cheerful, strident colouring.

Foxgloves. These don't mind a shady corner where few other plants will grow.

Perennials do not need much attention, but the taller plants will need a little support from bean sticks or garden canes. If, after three or four years, your plants seem to be losing some of their vigour, they can be given a new lease of life by being lifted, cleaned, divided and returned to the soil with a little fertilizer or manure.

Bulbs. By investing wisely in bulbs, you can make sure of a bright and cheerful display in early spring. (There are bulbs which flower in summer and autumn, too, but these are rivalled by so many other blooms.)

Taking a cutting

The plants shown in the nurseryman's catalogues under the heading 'Bulbs' usually include those which store nourishment in rhizomes or swollen stems (such as the iris), and those like the dahlia which use enlarged root stocks as reserves, as well as the true bulbs such as the daffodil, the narcissus and the tulip.

From your point of view, all these can be neatly divided into two separate categories:

Those that can be safely treated as perennials, and can be left in the ground for a number of years (daffodils, narcissi, snowdrops, crocuses, scillas, muscari, and many more).

Crocus corms

Those which should be lifted from the ground after they have flowered (tulips, gladioli, dahlias, etc).

Don't be tempted to trim the foliage off any bulb until it has withered and turned brown or yellow. If you do, you will be depriving the bulb of the nourishment it needs for its store.

To give the best possible results, all bulbs should be planted at the most propitious times of the year. These are:

Autumn (for bulbs that are to flower in the following spring)
Spring (for bulbs that are to flower in the summer)
Summer (for bulbs that are to flower in the autumn).

Don't plant your bulbs too deeply, or leave them so near the surface that mice and other pests can get at them. Measure roughly the depth of each bulb from tip to base and multiply this measurement by two. The resulting figure will indicate the depth of soil beneath which that bulb should lie. For example, a bulb one and a half inches thick should be buried three inches below the surface.

Shrubs. No one who has a garden of any size can afford to forget shrubs, since they need very little attention once they are established. Many shrubs are extremely decorative, and most can be relied on to produce a fine display of flowers at the appropriate season of the year. Among the easy-to-grow shrubs that can be recommended are:

Forsythia. Flowers profusely in the early spring—sometimes producing a blaze of bright yellow before the last snows of winter have been properly forgotten.

Broom. Not unlike gorse, but, fortunately, without the prickles, broom is found in a wide range of colours, from deep crimson to white.

Buddleia. Well-known for its sweet, honey-like scent, the buddleia will bring a variety of butterflies to your garden.

Cacti are very popular nowadays, because they are easy to grow, they come in a great variety of shapes, textures and silhouettes, and they bring a welcome suggestion of warm, dry far-away places to our everyday surroundings. They flourish best, in temperate climates, on a sunny window sill, but they can be taken outdoors in late spring or early summer, their pots being sunk up to the rim in the soil of a flowerbed or rockery. Here are some suggestions for successful cactus growing:

Pot each cactus in a container that looks much too small for it. Fill the bottom with broken crocks, for good drainage.

Use a mixture of rich loam and sand, in equal parts. Add a little leaf mould or charcoal, if you wish, but no fertilizer.

Rest each cactus for several months, during the winter. Put it in a cool room where it can catch any sunshine that may be going, but where the temperature will never drop below 40° Fahrenheit, even at night. Water it sparingly, once a month or so, with water that is at least room temperature.

Keep all cacti away from the fumes of domestic gas which will deprive the plants of oxygen and eventually kill them.

Tubs, urns and baskets. You can add lots of colour and interest to your garden, or to your back yard, by growing plants in tubs, urns, troughs and other suitable containers. Not only do these give additional accommodation for growing things, but they may also be used to raise some of your favourite plants to eye level, where you can enjoy them from an unusual angle.

It is important to see that any soil you put in a free-standing container has drainage facilities. Cover the bottom of the container with a layer of crocks—stones, flints, pieces of broken flowerpot, and the like—add a layer of leaf mould or peat if you have any, and then fill up with earth, or with a mixture of earth and a good potting compost.

It is important, too, to water the plants in a free-standing container regularly, for the soil can become dry very quickly. It can become impoverished quite quickly, too, so give it an occasional feed of liquid manure or a light sprinkling of bone meal or proprietary fertilizer.

Among the many delightful plants you can grow in tubs, urns and troughs are primulas, polyanthes, geraniums, hardy fuchsias, nasturtiums, and other hardy annuals. Miniature roses alone can make a most attractive display.

A wire hanging basket can be planted in late April or May so that it will make a most decorative feature throughout the summer. Pack the bottom and sides with a thick padding of sphagnum moss, which you can find growing in boggy areas on heaths, filling with a good mixture of loam and potting compost as you work upwards, and incorporating some trailing lobelia plants with their roots to the inside. Add nasturtiums if you want some more flamboyant effects, and plant the upper surface just as you would that in any other container. A basket garden of this kind can be a source of great pleasure especially for those unfortunate people who have no other facilities for growing plants.

Further reading

JANET DRYSDALE, *Gardens and Gardening* (Studio Vista).
C. A. LEJEUNE, *Enjoy Making A Garden out of Nothing* (Gollancz).
GERTRUDE JEKYLL, *On Gardening* (Studio Vista).

Gliding

There are just a few outdoor hobbies that you cannot hope to enjoy when pocket money is in short supply. Gliding is one of these. If you are in a position to pay some hundreds of pounds for an airworthy craft, if you have enough ground for storage and landing, and if you have enough kind friends to get you airborne you can go ahead more or less on your own. If you are short of any of these necessary factors you will have to join a club.

Finding out about clubs. There are at least sixty large and well-established gliding clubs in the British Isles, six of them being centred on Lasham, in Hampshire, and the rest being fairly well distributed over the land. Some of these are very well equipped and staffed; some are service clubs and are limited to members of HM Forces. There are also numerous minor clubs, kept going by small groups of devoted enthusiasts, but most of these only manage to operate at week-ends.

The best way to start gliding is, undoubtedly, to go on a short course at one of the best-organized clubs. These courses usually last a week or a fortnight and cost no more than most equally enjoyable holidays. Particulars of the clubs that run these courses can be obtained from the British Gliding Association, 19 Park Lane, London W1.

Gliding tuition is usually given in easy stages. First, you will probably be taken up as a passenger for air experience. The instructor will be flying the glider, and you may be sitting beside him. You will be able to observe how he checks all the equipment and controls before he starts the flight, and how the necessary signals are given to the helpers who are about to make the launch.

When you have made one or two of these 'trial flights' you will probably be allowed to handle the controls yourself for part of a flight. Your instructor will continue to handle the glider for the take-off and landing.

By the time the holiday is over, you will know for certain whether you want gliding to be your regular hobby or not. If you do, you will probably be able to arrange to become a member of the club you have been visiting. For a small yearly subscription, supplemented by a nominal fee for each flight, you will be able to experience all the joys of finding thermal upcurrents, and of using them to gain height, of map reading from the air, and of planning and carrying out long cross-country journeys successfully. You will have all the pleasure of flying, in fact, with a fraction of the expense.

Further reading
John Simpson, *Tackle Gliding This Way* (Stanley Paul).

Heraldry

Wherever you go, when you are out of doors, you will see heraldic decorations—on churches, castles, and other ancient buildings; outside colleges and schools; on inns and hostelries of all kinds; even on letter boxes and telephone kiosks. If you are interested in history, and if you want to develop your eye for design and colour, you will enjoy studying heraldry. It is a subject that has little practical use nowadays, but it can remind us most pleasurably of the romantic days when knights were bold, and when all good men were expected to be chivalrous.

Don't be put off, when you start, by the puzzling terms used by some of the more advanced authorities. There are a lot of complicated rules that have to be learned by people studying the subtler refinements of heraldry, and the language they use is often antiquated and obscure. But you can get a good working knowledge of heraldry without becoming bogged down in its finer technicalities. The first principles are quite easy to understand.

Originally, heraldry began as a means of identification. When different foods are put into metal containers that are all more or less the same size and shape, labels have to be stuck on to the outsides in case anyone chooses a tin with the wrong contents. Armour, unadorned, can be just as baffling. That is why distinctive marks or 'cognizances' were chosen after the twelfth century by knights entitled to bear arms. Each knight wanted a personal label by which he could be distinguished from other knights in the grim hurly-burly of battle, or in the picturesque proceedings of peace-time tournaments.

The methods of heraldry. Let us see, first, how a man might decorate his shield. Ordinarily, he would choose one of a number of recognized emblems, or 'charges', such as a 'pale' or vertical stripe, a 'bend' or diagonal stripe, or a 'chevron' or inverted V, and he would have this painted on the outer surface of the shield, or the 'field', where it would be seen at a glance by friend and foe alike. If you keep this procedure in mind, you will understand why early heraldic designs were usually quite simple, and why they normally consisted of colours superimposed on metals or metals on colours, which make an effective contrast, and only very rarely of colours on colours or metals on metals, which could be confusing.

You will understand, too, why only a small range of bold, unmistakable colours is used in heraldry—there would be no time to look for subtle shades and tints in the rough and tumble of battle. These are the five heraldic colours, with the intriguing names by which they are known:

Blue (Azure)   Red (Gules)   Green (Vert)   Purple (Purpure)
Black (Sable).

The two metals used are Gold (Or) and Silver (Argent). Artists often represent these by yellow and white respectively. Thus, you are quite likely to find a red lion rampant on a yellow or white field or background, but you are not likely to find it on green or purple unless it has been put there by someone with little knowledge of heraldry.

Observant people can often trace a lot of family history by looking at the arms on a shield. Arms were, and are, hereditary possessions —that is, the use of a knight's armorial bearings would pass by succession to his eldest son, together with his lands and his title. As a result, arms are closely associated with family pride, and the junior members of wealthy and powerful families frequently elected to bear the arms of the family's head, with some small changes or additions that were known as 'differences'. Even a small extra star near the top of a shield may be enough to indicate an exact family relationship to those 'in the know'.

Helmets. Above the shield, in a *full* heraldic 'achievement', you will find a helm or helmet. This, too, can tell you quite a lot about the man who owns the achievement:

> If he is a peer of the realm, he will have a barred helm of silver, decorated with gold, set in profile above the shield.

> If he is a baronet or a knight, he will have a steel helmet which is usually set full face, with its visor raised.

> If he is an esquire or an untitled gentleman he will have a closed steel helm, which is usually set in profile.

The use of different kinds of helm to show a bearer's rank was a comparatively recent innovation in heraldry. Until the time of the Stuart kings (1603-1714) there were no firm rules about this, so it is not safe to jump to conclusions when you are studying medieval or Tudor achievements.

Crests. On top of their helms, many men entitled to bear arms chose to fix special ornaments, or crests. At first, only kings and powerful nobles seem to have added crests to their achievements, but the habit of wearing them soon spread to people of less importance.

The earliest crests were quite small and light, and were made by folding pieces of leather or parchment so that they looked rather like the fans used by court ladies centuries later. A crest of this sort would be decorated in the same way as the bearer's shield and would help with the process of identification.

Later, crests became more ambitious, and would not necessarily be related in any way to the arms emblazoned on the shields. Animals, birds, mythical creatures, mystical symbols—any of these might be carved out of wood or fabricated with metal, leather or feathers and fixed to the top of a helm to provide extra colour and interest at the pinnacle of a knight's accoutrements. As a crest of this kind can be reproduced separately—say, on top of a gatepost, or on writing paper—it may be the best known part of a heraldic achievement.

Surcoats and mantling. In the thirteenth century, many knights wore surcoats over their armour to give them some protection from rain and the heat of the sun. These coats were usually embellished with the armorial bearings of the wearer, and they must have been extremely decorative and colourful. The term 'coat of arms' still survives, but nowadays it is applied to armorial bearings generally.

When the Crusaders arrived in the Holy Land, they found that the direct rays of the sun beating down on their unprotected helmets made them very uncomfortable, so they arranged extra pieces of cloth to hang down from below the crests. These drapings, which were known as 'mantlings' or 'lambrequins', would stream out splendidly behind like banners when the knights were riding at speed, and so they would be coloured, lined, and sometimes given decorative edgings to add to the general effect. You can see one of the most sumptuous mantlings of all—gold, lined with ermine—in the Royal Arms borne by Queen Elizabeth I and all British Sovereigns after her.

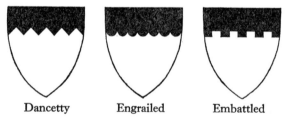

| Dancetty | Engrailed | Embattled |

These drawings show three of the many ways in which a heraldic line may be given variety

Badges and supporters. When you examine the Royal Arms closely, you may wonder how the lion and the unicorn came to be included, one on each side of the central shield. Animals, birds, mythical beasts and human beings placed like this are known as 'supporters', and like the rules that control the design and placing of helms they arrived comparatively late in the history of heraldry.

To understand the origin of supporters, one has to remember that a man entitled to bear arms could not bestow them on his servants, or on the soldiers under his command. They were his own personal possession, and if he wanted a mark of ownership, or overlordship, he had to have some other and quite different emblem, which was usually known as a 'badge'. If he chose (say) a lion or a unicorn as his badge, he could have it painted, embroidered or stamped on all his belongings and on the uniforms of his retainers, and he would almost certainly include it in the personal seal with which he authenticated all his documents.

Occasionally a man would have more than one lordship, and, therefore, more than one badge. When two badges were included in a seal, one would be placed on each side of the central shield. Then, it would be only a small step to the incorporation of the badges in the personal arms as flankers, upholders or supporters of the shield. Hence the beasts in the Royal Arms!

The motto. Most men entitled to bear arms would choose to include their personal motto, or that of their family, in their achievement. Some mottos took the form of a pun on the family name, others expressed noble sentiments, a few were boastful or threatening. The motto would usually be inscribed on a decorative ribbon or 'escroll' under the shield.

Signs and hatchments. Once you have learned how a heraldic achievement is made up, you will be keen to see as many authentic examples as possible. Here are some of the best places to look for them:

Inn signs are often heraldic in character, the word 'Arms' being commonly incorporated in the name of a place of refreshment. In some cases, the original landlord may have been a man entitled to wear the badge of a local landowner or nobleman. He would be eager to associate his establishment with a source of powerful patronage. In other cases, the inn may have been visited by some great nobleman on one of his journeys. It was not unusual for a notable person to have his arms displayed outside a temporary stopping place, and, occasionally, an escutcheon would be left behind as a token of appreciation for excellent service. Such names as the 'Red Lion', the 'Feathers' and the 'Rose and Crown' are undoubtedly heraldic in origin.

Hatchments are still to be seen in many churches. These were large lozenge-shaped panels or canvases, usually in a black frame. On a hatchment, there would be painted the heraldic achievement of an important person, and when that person died the hatchment would be hung up over the door of his or her home until the time of the funeral. Then it would be carried in the funeral procession and put up in the church in which the person was buried until it could be replaced with a permanent memorial. Sometimes a hatchment was not removed and can still be seen hanging in the quiet obscurity of a rural chancel or belfry. The rules of hatchment-making were just as clearly defined as the processes of the other branches of heraldry. If a man died before his wife, for example,

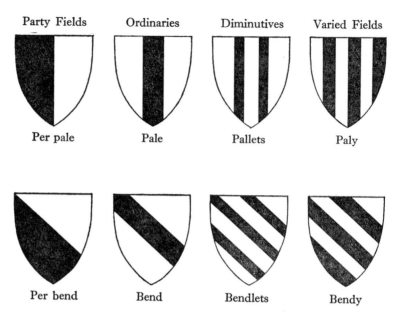

Party Fields	Ordinaries	Diminutives	Varied Fields
Per pale	Pale	Pallets	Paly
Per bend	Bend	Bendlets	Bendy

These are some of the simpler forms and fields you may come across

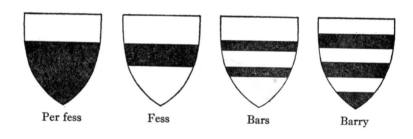

Per fess	Fess	Bars	Barry

the dexter (or right hand) half of the background would be painted black and the sinister (or left hand) half would be painted white. If a woman died before her husband, the sinister side of her hatchment would be painted black and the dexter side would be painted white. When the terms 'sinister' and 'dexter' are used in heraldry, the sides of the shield are named as they would be seen *from the back*, that is, by a person holding the shield.

The heralds. In the twelfth and early thirteenth centuries the choice of bearings was largely a matter of luck—a knight would select a cognizance and the colour with which he wanted it painted, without knowing for certain whether any other knight outside his immediate neighbourhood had already hit on the same combination.

Then the heralds began to give a certain amount of guidance in the matter. These were men who made their living by travelling about arranging tournaments and organizing the events when they actually took place, and it was to their advantage to be able to recognize all the knights taking part without any possibility of confusion. So, they evolved a system by which the various parts of an achievement could be described briefly in words, and recorded, and they took it upon themselves to see that there was no duplication. Today, armorial records are kept by the members of the Heralds' College, who occupy a handsome building in Queen Victoria Street, London, that was designed for them after the Great Fire. The Officers of the College are members of the Royal Household, and are experts on State Ceremonial.

Blazonry. A verbal description of an armorial bearing is known as a 'blazon', and it may amuse you to study the system that the medieval heralds developed. It is still in use today!

First, the field or background of the shield is described, with its 'tincture' (colour or metal) and the way in which it has been subdivided or given a texture. Then the principal ordinary or charge is called up, with any qualifications that may be necessary, and its tincture. Finally, any lesser charges, with their tinctures, are described.

As an example, you might find that the bearings on a shield were described something like these, of Berkeley:

Gules semy of crosslets formy, a chevron argent.

In layman's language this might be interpreted:

On a red background (Gules), there are scattered (semy of) some small crosses, each of which has arms that increase in width (crosslets formy) and a silver chevron, or inverted V.

Heraldry as a hobby. Heraldry was evolved during a period when stately pageantry was part of the pattern of life. You may be wondering how it can make a satisfying hobby in the fast moving mechanized twentieth century. The answer to that lies in the continuing interest taken in heraldry by all kinds of people—today, clubs, societies and commercial undertakings as well as private individuals, are eager to acquire armorial bearings. You are as likely to find examples worth studying in a new block of shops and offices as you are in a medieval parish church.

To equip yourself for researches into heraldry you will need only a sketch book or small album and a pencil or pen. With these you can record quite adequately all the bearings you come across, though

Marriages can be indicated heraldically by grouping the arms of husband and wife together. *Above* by impalement, *below* by dimidiation, or combining exact halves

you may decide to carry coloured pencils, or inks, or water colours as well to add the decorative tinctures that make heraldic achievements so attractive to look at, and to have around. You will also need access to a few good books on heraldry, which will help you to understand what you are seeing. Three of the best are included in the list below.

Further reading
C. W. SCOTT-GILES, *Looking at Heraldry* (Phoenix House).
C. BOUTELL, *Heraldry, Ed. by C. W. Scott-Giles* (Frederick Warne).
IAIN MONCRIEFFE, *Simple Heraldry* (Thomas Nelson).

Kite-making and kite-flying

Flying a kite you have bought at a shop ready-made may be fun—and even exciting, in difficult weather conditions—but for the greatest satisfaction there is nothing like flying a kite that you have made with your own hands. Any experiments you make with mass-produced box or pegtop kites may, therefore, be regarded as preliminaries to the real task—that of getting airborne, and keeping airborne, a kite you have constructed to your own less conventional specifications. Here is how you can set about it.

The history of kite-flying. First, you should know a little about the history of kites, so that you will see what fantastic possibilities may be open to you if you use a little resourcefulness.

It is fairly well established that kites were being flown in China at least three centuries before the birth of Christ. They were used for various purposes, being designed to carry ropes over gorges that were due to be bridged, for shining lights into inaccessible places, and for raising wind-operated musical instruments. By the end of the Manchu Dynasty, man-lifting kites had been developed, and were used for reconnaissance and other purposes in time of war. Kites have also been used in various parts of the world for ship-to-shore rescue preparations, for pulling boats, and for drawing carriages along the public highway. It is quite wrong to think of them merely as amusing toys!

How kites overcome gravity. Next, you should give some thought to the ways in which kites, which are heavier than air, can be made to climb upwards away from the earth by the careful manipulation of an operator's line. At least four important factors have to be borne in mind:

Resistance to air. If you hold a postcard in a horizontal position, and then move it sideways, it will travel through the air with the greatest possible ease. If you hold it vertically, and then try to move it at exactly the same speed, it will encounter greater air resistance, and you will have to push a little bit harder. The angles at which the flat surfaces of a kite are presented to an airstream are extremely important.

Upward thrust. You may appreciate the importance of this even more if you put a piece of paper on a table and then blow along the supporting surface towards it. If the air current you make is strong enough, the paper will be lifted from the table as it moves away from you. You will make use of this factor, which is usually known as 'upward thrust', when you are launching your kites. By pulling a kite forward against the wind you will be able to make its front or leading edge climb gradually into the air, creating, as you do so, a partial vacuum above its upper surface which will help the kite to rise.

Propulsion. This is the force that you, as the operator, will exert as you tighten your line. As you do this—perhaps by pulling, perhaps by running into the wind—the kite should move forwards, and upwards, as wind resistance is converted into upward thrust.

To keep a kite flying steadily, it is essential that the forces exerted by resistance, upward thrust and propulsion should meet or intersect at the kite's *centre of gravity*—that is, the point in the kite round which the whole weight is evenly distributed. You may have to make several adjustments (perhaps altering the position of the kite line or lengthening or shortening the kite's tail) before any kite is satisfactorily balanced, and stable in flight.

Tools for kite-making. Most of the tools you will need for kite-making can be found in any home workshop. They include:

A hacksaw or tenon saw
A hammer (a 'pin' hammer is recommended)
A sharp penknife, X-Acto knife, or steel-backed razor blade
A small screwdriver
A wheel brace, with $\frac{1}{16}$ in., $\frac{3}{32}$ in., and $\frac{1}{8}$ in. dia. drills.

Other tools and items of equipment you are likely to have around, such as a fine file, an awl, a foot rule, a pencil and a pair of scissors may all prove useful.

Materials for kite-making. Almost any light, strong wood can be used for kite-making as long as it is flexible enough to withstand the shock of a sudden descent to the ground. Most shops that sell materials for model-makers sell suitable stripwoods in various lengths and thicknesses.

Garden canes are often used for kite-making because they are both strong and flexible. 'Centre' cane, made from the rattan palm, may be used to produce any part of a kite's profile which has pronounced curves, and cannot, therefore, be made with stronger, stiffer materials.

For covering your kites, you have quite a wide choice of materials, ranging from real silk (which was probably used by the original Chinese kite-makers) to tissue paper, which is light but easily torn. You will probably find a fine calico or cambric cloth or a strong kraft paper a better buy than either of the alternatives just mentioned—at least until you have had a lot of experience.

For fastening the component parts of your kite together, you will need a strong adhesive. Most of the proprietary animal or fish glues sold for model-making are suitable, and so are the excellent adhesives derived from polyvinyl acetate. If you are offered cellulose cements, use only the slower-drying 'high strength' varieties.

You will need string for bracing your kites, as well as for making bridles and for use as your kite line. There is a wide choice. Ordinary linen tent thread may be used for all general purposes when the kite is a small one, and is not to be flown at a greater height than 100 yards. Nylon fishing line is splendid—get line with 10 lb breaking strain for very small kites, and line with 25 lb breaking strain for the 3- and 4-footers. Don't use line that is any thicker than necessary or its weight will tend to drag the kite down.

A simple flat kite. In the illustration overleaf you will see how a flat 'trapezoidal' kite can be made very easily.

Use a piece of $\frac{3}{8}$ in. × $\frac{3}{8}$ in. stripwood for the spine. Thirty-six inches is a standard length and easily obtained. The spar, which may also be 36 in. long, can be made of stripwood, too, though if you have a good choice of woods, a slightly thinner section for the spar ($\frac{3}{8}$ in. × $\frac{1}{4}$ in.) would be preferable.

First, smooth down both members with sandpaper to remove any roughness which may weaken the cover when it is in position.

Then drill small holes near the end of the sticks to accommodate the frame string. (In some kites, it is better to cut V-shaped notches in the ends of the cross-members.) Find the exact centre of each, and make sure that it will balance correctly if poised on a knife-edge at this point.

Join the spine and the spar at their crossing point with glue, and bind the joint tightly with thin cord. It is not safe to notch or recess either of the members in this kind of crossing joint or you will weaken the structure at the point of greatest strain.

Then thread the frame-string through the holes, giving it a half turn around the wooden member of each hole. Tie the ends together at the bottom of the spine, leaving an inch or two extra to hang free so that you can attach a 'tail' to it eventually.

To plan the cover, put the frame on the paper or material you intend to use and mark out the shape with a soft pencil. Allow a margin $1\frac{1}{2}$ in. wide all round, and cut out.

Put some glue along the spine, press it down on to the cover, and leave it to dry. Then fold the margins over the frame-string, trimming them where necessary and glue them down to the back of the cover. If you are handy with a needle and thread you will probably choose to sew your cloth covers in position.

Making a bridle. A 'bridle' is a cord or combination of cords by which a flying line is joined to a kite. Most kites perform better if they are fitted with a bridle, since it is important that the operator shall be able to adjust quickly and easily the angle at which the kite is presented to the wind.

Attach a bridle to the flat kite shown by piercing the cover at the points indicated in the illustration. The cover will need reinforcing at these points. This can be done by gluing thin cardboard washers round the holes you have made.

The flying line can be attached to the bridle with a reef knot and a bowline knot, or by means of a small ring or washer (this is often referred to as a 'towing ring'). When you are satisfied that your kite

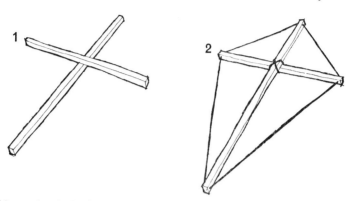

Making a simple flat kite
1 Fix spar to spine   2 Add framestrings

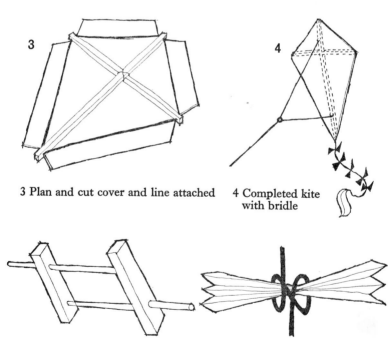

3 Plan and cut cover and line attached   4 Completed kite with bridle

Left A useful and easily made winder, *Right* The clove hitch, used for making the kite's tail

is correctly 'dressed' you can fix the relative positions of the bridle and the flying line with small strips of adhesive tape.

A kite's tail. Kites don't have tails just as decorative additions. Though a tail may add considerably to the appearance of an otherwise plain flat kite, it also improves its performance.

To prepare a tail that will steady a flat kite without adding much undesirable weight, take a piece of string 6 ft or 8 ft long and tie some folded strips of paper to it at 6 in. intervals. The clove hitch is a good knot to use for this.

Making a box kite. A simple box kite is quite easy to make. An elementary framework is shown in the illustration on this page.

Use four pieces of $\frac{3}{8}$ in. × $\frac{3}{8}$ in. stripwood each 36 in. long, for the longerons and eight pieces of $\frac{3}{8}$ in. × $\frac{3}{8}$ in. stripwood, each 12 in. long, for the crosspieces. Make the butt joints with glue and panel pins, and give them real permanence by binding some glued thread round them.

A box kite of this kind needs bracing, but wooden crossbraces may add disastrously to its weight. Instead, use strong thread or nylon line, starting at one of the junctions in the framework, winding it round two of the other longerons, and finishing so that it is quite taut with a knot at the fourth longeron. Do this at both ends of the kite, and then fix the thread finally in position with a little glue wherever it touches a spine.

Then add the frame-strings, as shown in the illustration.

Finally, cover the kite. Use any suitable material, but make sure that it is quite taut. A box kite with a floppy cover will never fly successfully.

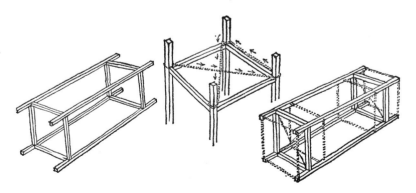

Left An easily constructed frame for a box kite, *Mid.* This shows how the box kite can be braced, *Right* The frame strings are added

111

A winder. All kite lines but the very shortest should be accommodated on a winder—you will not be able to pull in a hundred yards of line in a short time and keep it from tangling with your hands alone.

An old fishing reel fastened to a piece of wood (which acts as a handle) makes an excellent winder. If you do not have a large enough reel, make a simple winding device out of two pieces of stripwood and two pieces of circular dowelling. The shape is shown in the illustration on page 110.

Launching a kite. Under normal circumstances, it is fairly easy to put a kite into the air, especially if there are two people to co-operate in the launch—one to hold the kite up at arm's length, the other to supply the necessary gentle pull, and to pay out the line as the kite starts to rise.

It may not be quite so easy to make a quick launch if you are alone, but this is a satisfactory method:

First choose a spot where there will be no interference from trees or overhead wires.

Unwind some thirty or forty feet of line and lay it in a straight line on the ground. Try to arrange it in the direction of the wind.

Next place your winder on some raised surface so that you can pick it up easily as you pass.

Take up the kite and raise it above your head with one hand, holding the line in your other hand.

Then walk back along the line you have laid out, paying it out through your fingers as soon as the kite is exerting a strong pull.

When you reach the winder you can go on paying out more line from that, as the kite continues to rise.

Precautions. A large kite on a long line can be a menace to safety unless certain precautions are taken. Here are a few suggestions:

Sore hands. A kite line running at speed through the fingers can cause serious cuts or burns. The remedy for this, of course, is to wear thick gloves!

Lightning. A kite line can act as a lightning conductor—that is why metal lines are not recommended. It is advisable to wind in all kites if there seems to be any possibility of a storm.

The Law. In some districts, there are bye-laws that control kite-flying. If you want to keep out of trouble, make a few discreet enquiries before you send up your first kite.

Further reading

CLIVE HART, *Your Book of Kites* (Faber and Faber).

HAROLD RIDGWAY, *Kite Making and Flying* (Arco Publications).

Oil painting

If you enjoy sketching in pencil, and if you like adding interest to your drawings with washes of water colour, why not try oil painting? Tackled in the right way, it is a splendid hobby that need not be expensive. Let us look first at each of the main items of equipment—colours, canvases, brushes, vehicles and a palette—in turn.

Top Palettes. *Bottom left* Palette knives *Bottom mid.* Oilpainting brushes—flat, filbert and round *Right* A light, portable, folding easel, invaluable for painting out of doors

Colours. Oil paints are usually sold ready mixed, or 'ground', in collapsible tubes. You will be offered 'students' colours', which are quite adequate for your early efforts, and 'artists' quality', which are more expensive, usually more finely ground, and preferable for work that is expected to last for centuries!

There are literally dozens of different colours from which to choose, whichever grade you decide to use. If you bear in mind that the greatest colourists have always used a restricted palette, allowing themselves only an easily controllable range of permanent and compatible colours, you will be following a sound tradition, as well as being economical.

White. You will need more white paint than any other, since you will not be able to dilute your colours with water when you want to produce pale tints, as you can when you are using an ordinary child's paintbox. Flake white, or white lead, is very popular. It dries well, and makes a strong, leathery skin of pigment, but it is rather poisonous. Zinc white takes longer to dry, and has a tendency to crack, but is safer to use. Titanium white was unknown to the Old Masters, but it is non-poisonous, brilliantly white, and no more expensive than the others in most manufacturers' lists.

The earth colours. There is a splendid range of yellows, reds and browns made originally from natural earths. They are not very bright, but they are cheap, pleasant to use, and absolutely permanent. Take your pick from these, and you will have a sound basis for a palette for painting outdoors:

Yellow ochre. A smooth, dull yellow that is extremely useful for mixing the subtle duns and greens of pasture and heathland.

Raw umber and burnt umber. Irreplaceable browns. The raw earth has an attractive greenish tinge; burnt umber is a strong chocolate.

Raw sienna and burnt sienna. Not all artists like these—the raw earth, because it is usually ground in a high proportion of oil; the burnt earth, because its colour tends to vary according to the source of the supply.

Indian red and light red. Useful colours that may be reminiscent of the soft tones of terracotta or old brickwork. Light red tends to be variable, like burnt sienna.

More brilliant yellows. You will probably need a brighter yellow than yellow ochre when you are painting out of doors. Lemon yellow is as clean as a fresh primrose, and reasonably permanent. Cadmium yellow, the best alternative, has a slight tendency towards orange.

Oranges and reds. None of the earth colours are anything like as bright as the colours of the rainbow. If you need oranges and reds that are relatively pure, you can experiment with cadmium orange, cadmium red and cadmium scarlet. Alizarin scarlet and alizarin crimson are satisfactory alternatives, but as it is not safe to mix them with ultramarine they are not universal favourites. Vermilion is beautifully vivid, but it tends to become badly discoloured when exposed to city air.

Greens. For soft, subtle greens try terre verte, which was, when it was originally made, a transparent earth colour with a high oil content. Viridian, or transparent green oxide of chromium, is a comparatively recent addition to the colour box, but it is one of the most useful hues, and once you have tried it you will probably come to rely on it.

Blues. Real ultramarine is rich and permanent, but it is one of the most expensive colours made. French ultramarine is a cheap artificial substitute that is in most respects entirely satisfactory. Cerulean blue and cobalt blue are preferred by some artists, but they tend to be more expensive. In the blue green range comes Prussian blue, one of the most powerful colours on the market. With Prussian blue and viridian on your palette you should be able to tackle any landscape without being defeated by the richness of the vegetation.

Blacks. There is not much to choose between lamp black and ivory black, which are both cheap, slightly transparent and reasonably durable. Blue black is not so intense as either of these, but with it you can produce many subtle and attractive greys.

If you find it difficult to choose between all the colours listed here, try painting with these only on your palette:

Titanium white, yellow ochre, light red, cobalt blue, ivory black. You can add further colours, to extend your range of possible mixings, when you have explored the resources of a few.

Canvases. Canvases that have been commercially prepared are sold ready for use on tongued and grooved wooden stretchers. The best grades make splendid supports for painting on, but they tend to be rather expensive, so if your pocket money is limited you may prefer to try one of these alternatives, at least for the sketches you make while you are gaining experience.

Sketching boards. These are light, flat boards, surfaced with cloth or given a texture that resembles cloth. They can be obtained in a wide range of sizes and are comparatively cheap.

Hardboard, wallboard and strawboard. These are even cheaper, but as they are usually rather porous and strong in tone when they are marketed you will have to be prepared to apply some priming, and a ground. To do this successfully, you will have to understand the functions of each.

A priming is a preparation, usually liquid, that is used to make a surface a little less absorbent. An unprimed board or canvas may soak up the oil from any paints that are put on it, until they look sparse and chalky. The oil may make the support rot quickly, too. These unpleasant consequences can be avoided if you apply a coat of size or very thin glue. To prepare the size, soak one sheet in cold water overnight, to soften it, then pour the cold water away and substitute for it a large teacupful of boiling water. Stir until the size has dissolved. Powdered size and glue can be dissolved in hot water to a similar consistency.

A ground is an opaque covering applied to a primed surface to change its colour or texture before it is painted on. It will consist of some inert substance, such as slaked plaster, builders' whiting, or powdered white lead, which is ground up in a permanently retentive fluid or mixture of fluids.

A good quality white lead paint makes an excellent ground, though you will have to plan well ahead if you decide to use it, since each coat must be given at least a week to dry before the next is applied.

Gesso, too, is quite easy to prepare and apply. Make a binding solution by dissolving some size or glue in boiling water so that the resulting liquid feels just slightly sticky when tested between the fingers. Then stir some fine slaked plaster into this, adding enough to make a mixture that has the consistency of thin cream. (Plaster can be slaked by being stirred for twenty minutes or so in a bucketful of clean water. At the end of that time it can be safely allowed to settle at the bottom.) Whiting can be used instead of slaked plaster, but it makes a slightly coarser ground.

Use a soft, wide, flat brush to apply a ground to a canvas or panel. Move the brush in one direction only when you are applying the first coat. When this has had a chance to dry, apply a further coat, keeping the brush moving at right angles to the first direction. It is safer to apply several coats of thin gesso than one thick coat. A final coat of very thin size will make a ground less absorbent.

Sometimes, you may feel like starting a painting on a canvas or panel with a toned ground, that is, one to which a little colour has been added. This is quite permissible—Constable painted some charming landscapes on panels the colour of a cigar box—but oil paints tend to become more transparent with the passage of time, so a toned ground can hardly fail to have a darkening effect.

A palette. Before you can start painting you will need a flat, smooth surface on which to mix your colours. A table top is often used in indoor studios: for outdoor painting you will have to provide yourself with a light and portable palette. It will have to be properly balanced, too—if it isn't, your hand will soon get tired!

All purveyors of artists' materials stock palettes in the traditional shapes that have been evolved through centuries of hard use. Instead of buying one of these you may find it more convenient to cut yourself a rectangular palette out of a sheet of thick plywood—preferably one that will fit into the lid of the box in which you are going to carry your paints. It should have a thumb hole near one of the short ends, and this should be chamfered, so that there are no hard corners to bear uncomfortably on your thumb.

Oil a new palette thoroughly before you use it—rub several coats of linseed oil into the wood, letting two or three days elapse for drying between each application.

Brushes. Brushes sold for oil painting can be roughly divided into two categories—stiff brushes, made with hog hair or hog bristle, and soft brushes, made with sable and similar hairs. Buy only a few if you are a beginner, and then add to your collection when experience has shown you what other types you need.

Hog-hair brushes are usually made in sizes that range from No. 1 (the smallest) to No. 12 (very large). The four shapes most often encountered are long flat, short flat, round, and filbert. Invest in as good-quality brushes as you can afford—brushes made with inferior bristles soon lose their resilience when they are charged with paint.

116

Sable brushes are useful for painting flat, thin areas of colour, and for adding fine details, but they are not tough enough to be used for mixing stiff paints, or for 'scumbling' dry colours over a bone-hard undercoat. Ideally, you should have hog-hair brushes as well as sables in your equipment.

Palette knives. For manipulating the colours on a palette you will need one of the flat, flexible knives made specially for the purpose. A palette knife with a blade that tapers towards a small rounded 'point' will be easiest to handle. Palette knives are sometimes used instead of brushes for applying paint to canvases.

Vehicles. A vehicle is a liquid or mixture of liquids used to dilute oil colour, to bind pigments together, and to make them easier to blend. Most of the oil paints you buy will have been ground in a lot of poppy oil, which is slow drying, and is intended to keep the colours from solidifying while they are still in the tubes. You may like to leave all colours on a piece of blotting paper for a few minutes, to remove any excess of oil, before transferring them to your palette.

Working vehicles can be roughly divided into these categories:

First, there are the 'thin' essences and spirits such as turpentines and petrol. These are excellent for the preliminary laying in of a picture, and give a pleasant, matt surface on which slightly oilier coats may be superimposed. The specially purified turpentine sold by the suppliers of artists' materials is rather expensive, but the lighter fuel used by smokers is quite satisfactory, and relatively cheap.

Then there are the fatter vehicles such as linseed oil, poppy oil and nut oil. Linseed oil makes a tough and leathery skin if it is allowed to dry out thoroughly over the course of several months, and poppy oil dries more slowly even than that; nut oil is preferred by some artists, but it is relatively expensive. A satisfactory vehicle can be made by mixing linseed oil and spirits of turpentine in equal quantities.

Varnish mixtures and wax mixtures should be left for the experts to use, however tempting they may sound when described in the catalogues.

Dippers. These are small metal containers used for holding painting vehicles. The best type of dipper is fitted with a small metal clip on the underside, by which it can be attached to the palette, and a turned over lip that will minimize spilling.

You will also need one or two small glass or plastic vessels to contain turpentine substitute, petrol or paraffin, which you can use for keeping your brushes clean. At the end of a day's painting, use a little soap and water to clear the paint away from the roots of the hairs or bristles of each of the brushes you have been using. Some clean rag will be useful for removing the excess moisture.

117

Easels. You will find a folding easel that is compact and portable a great asset when you are painting out of doors. For two or three guineas you can buy an easel that is both light and easy to erect. Don't be tempted to buy an easel with a lot of extraneous gadgets or you will spend most of your time setting it up and packing it away.

Choosing a subject. When you are sufficiently well equipped you will be eager to go out and start painting. Then you will be faced with the problem of choosing a suitable subject. These are some of the factors you should bear in mind if you want your sketching trips to be truly successful, as well as enjoyable:

The sun. Don't set up your easel in front of a picturesque landscape or charming group of old buildings if the sun is likely to shine down directly into your eyes as soon as you start work. The sun's glare can be especially disturbing during the fine intervals in showery weather, so remember its position even when it is temporarily hidden behind a cloud.

The wind. Strong gusts of wind can be just as disturbing as sunshine, so choose a sheltered spot for your easel if you possibly can. If the subject you want to paint can only be studied from an exposed position, try anchoring the legs of your easel to the ground with the heaviest stones you can find. It's no joke to have a canvas covered with wet oil paint flying around in the teeth of an unexpected squall!

Farm animals (and their custodians) can sometimes prove a nuisance to landscape painters. Get permission from the owner or occupier of the land before you start, and you will be warned of any possible pitfalls—as, for example, the imminent arrival of the stock bull in the field you have chosen as your painting pitch.

When you are sure that the position you have chosen is satisfactory, you will have to decide how much of the prospect before you is going to be included in your canvas. You may find a viewfinder useful as a rough guide while you are establishing the composition of your picture. To make one, cut a small rectangular hole in a piece of cardboard and then hold it up in front of your subject. By moving it backwards and forwards, up and down, and to right and left you will be able to see in isolation the features that are going to make up your picture, and you will find the screen-like effect of the hole a splendid aid to concentration.

Painting a picture. Before you can start painting in earnest you will have to arrange your palette, so squeeze out near the edge a little of each of the colours you have decided to use. When you are working at speed you will find it helpful to know exactly where each colour is, so you should always lay them out, as far as possible, in the same order.

118

There are several different ways in which you can begin an oil painting. Some artists like to use thin sticks of charcoal for a preliminary 'lay in'. Others like to use thin washes of colour, liberally diluted with petrol or turpentine. It is not satisfactory to use a pencil for drawing preliminary outlines, because the graphite will make the colours placed over it seem stained and smeary.

As your painting develops, you will be faced with a number of the problems that beset all artists—the difficulty of representing trees, for example, so that they look as if they have really grown, and the puzzles of perspective. You will find the answers to a number of these problems if you read about sketching outdoors on pages 169–179 of this book.

Usually a small landscape sketch painted with oil colours will be most satisfactory if it is completed in one day. If you find it necessary to work on a sketch for several days you can remove surplus oils and provide an excellent basis for the next day's work by pressing a sheet of absorbent paper over the surface of your canvas before you pack up for the night.

If you find it difficult to carry your wet canvases home without damaging your clothes or those of the people with whom you are travelling, try fixing two canvases together, face to face, with the canvas pins sold specially for the purpose. These consist of small wooden distance pieces, to keep the canvases apart, each distance piece being fitted with two sharp metal spikes that hold it in place.

Varnishing. Because oil paint goes hard in a matter of days once it has been applied to a canvas, many people think that an oil painting is complete and ready for varnishing almost as soon as it is taken off the artist's easel. Unfortunately, the chemical changes that take place when oil paints are exposed to air are a great deal slower than this, and a film of pigment may not be completely inert until several months have elapsed. If you want to give one of your paintings a protective coat of varnish any sooner than this—as for example, if you want to give it greater brilliance and luminosity before you send it to an exhibition—use retouching varnish, which will not seal off the underlying coats of paint finally and completely. If you can bear to wait, you can use copal varnish or mastic varnish instead.

Copal varnish is made by dissolving a hard resin in linseed oil or some other drying oil. It will protect the surface of your painting from the harmful action of moisture, gases and dirt. It is more substantial and permanent than mastic varnish, but if anything goes wrong it is extremely difficult to remove.

Mastic varnish is a spirit varnish. If it becomes dirty or discoloured it can usually be removed without damage to the underlying paint surfaces, but this is not a procedure that any experts would recommend.

Whichever varnish you use (and it is not, strictly speaking, necessary to use any) choose a bright, warm day for the operation when the humidity is low. Work in a dust-free place, using a large flat, soft brush. Just before you apply the varnish give the paint surface a final light rub with a scrap of clean rag that you have dipped in fresh lighter fuel, and protect the varnished surface from dust and draughts for forty-eight hours at least before you show it, proudly, to your friends.

Further reading
GUY R. WILLIAMS, *Enjoy Painting in Oils* (Gollancz).

Pets

'No family is complete without at least one pet'. This is often said, and it seems to be true, for tame animals and birds can be relied on to add pleasure and interest to the sometimes monotonous daily routine. Even a slow-moving reptile such as a tortoise may have its own peculiar charm, though it may not be as immediately appealing, or as responsive, as a warm-blooded creature such as a dormouse or a bush baby.

Of course, all pets impose certain responsibilities on their owners. They have to be housed properly, fed regularly with the correct diet, kept clean, and possibly, groomed, and tended when they are sick. For that reason, all young people should learn how to look after animals—possibly by sharing the ownership of one—before they take on a pet of their own.

It is not always easy to divide pets into 'Pets for Indoors' and 'Pets for Outdoors', because not many pets fall neatly into either of these categories. A donkey, for instance, would be allotted by most people to the field and farmyard, but at least one small donkey has lived a very happy life in a bedroom in a London hotel, enjoying its jaunts to the gardens in the nearby square as much as a child enjoys a trip to a sweetshop! A goat, on the other hand, can be assigned fairly safely to 'outdoors'. In border-line cases, it has seemed best to include the candidate with the fresh air addicts described in these pages, though your cat and your dog may often seem most reluctant to be taken away from the fireside!

Bantams

If you have a garden with a reasonably large lawn, you might like to consider keeping bantams. Although they are only like very small domestic fowls, bantams have considerable charm, and some of the varieties, the Silver and Gold Sebrights, for instance, with lovely lace-like feathers, are as decorative as any pet you could choose, bar the super-spectacular peacock and the magnificent ornamental pheasants, such as the Lady Amherst.

Don't let any bantams you buy wander unwatched in your garden unless you are quite sure that it is free from rats and other marauders. You can buy a suitable home for them, with an easily movable run and a little 'house' with nesting boxes, or you can make one, if you are reasonably handy, with some pieces of wood and wire netting. Ideally, your bantams should be allowed to range over a fresh area of grass each day. If they have to be confined, sprinkle sawdust or peat on the floor of their quarters, and change it before it has had a chance to become foul.

Bantams' eggs, though miniature, are well worth cooking, because they are delightfully rich. When a bantam hen has been laying for some time, she will probably develop a tendency to stay on her nest. This means that she is becoming broody. If you move her to a coop on her own, and give her two or three 'pot' eggs to sit on, you will soon be able to take these away and substitute real, fertile eggs for her to hatch. After twenty days, put a little luke-warm water on the shells of the eggs as this will help the chicks to break through the leathery skin that is sealing them in.

Bantams may be fed on wheat, maize and poultry mash. They also need fine grit and oyster shell and plenty of fresh clean water, just like ordinary domestic fowls. If a broody hen seems unwilling to leave her nest to take nourishment, lift her off gently by easing your hand underneath her, and then offer her some maize. If you don't do this she will lose weight and become unhealthy.

Cats

A kitten is one of the most playful and amusing creatures in the world, so it is not surprising that a cat sleeping on the hearth-rug has become, for most people, an integral part of the home! If you haven't a cat already, and if you would like to own one, you will not find it difficult to acquire a suitable pet, for 'queens' (as female cats are called) are very productive, and there is usually an unwanted litter of kittens somewhere in each district at any one time. You may have to pay quite a high price for a kitten from an exhibition or pedigree strain. Most mongrel kittens are virtually given away.

Go and see the kittens with their mother if you can, before you make your final choice. You will then be able to see what kind of animals the youngsters are likely to grow into (remember that a long-haired cat may need rather more care and grooming than a short-haired specimen) and you may be able to pick the liveliest member of the litter, which is the one that is likely to be the healthiest and the strongest. A kitten should be about eight or nine weeks old, and completely weaned, before it is removed from its mother.

You will probably be asked whether you want a male or a female kitten, and the answer you give will depend on whether you want your pet, in turn, to produce families when it has grown up! It is advisable to have a male cat neutered by a properly qualified vet. when it is about three months old if you want to be sure that it will not cause distress in the home by its smell and habits. Female cats can be 'spayed' by a vet or at an animal clinic if families are not wanted. This is a slightly more serious operation, but a healthy cat will usually get over it satisfactorily within a week.

When you get your kitten home, you will probably be tempted to play with it (or to let it play with you) until it is quite exhausted, but if it is to grow up healthily it must have a warm, comfortable, draught-proof bed where it can get plenty of sleep. If the weather is cold you may need to give it some extra warmth during its first few days away from its mother. A hot water bottle, wrapped in several thicknesses of blanket, will provide a nice warm glow without being dangerously hot.

A kitten will need a sanitary tray, too, until it is old enough to be allowed to spend a lot of its time outdoors. Such a tray should be made of metal or plastic, not wood, and it should be filled with dry sand, fresh earth, or one of the patent litters sold for the purpose at most pet shops. The tray should be emptied and refilled at least once each day. Twice a week you should wash it out with some disinfectant. The kitten will soon learn what the tray is for if you move it there when there are signs that the need is urgent.

When it is first weaned a kitten needs four meals a day, and these should be provided as nearly as possible at the same times each day. It can be given tepid milk, puppy food, boiled fish without bones, chopped cooked meat, finely shredded or diced vegetables, and proprietary cat foods. Raw meat is not a suitable food for young cats, but a few drops of cod liver oil may be added to a meal if it is thought that a kitten needs a little extra nourishment. Clean cold water should always be available, whatever the weather.

If you have a female cat which is about to have a family, you will usually be able to tell where she intends to make her nursery by watching her carefully during the last few days before the kittens arrive. The matter is something of a lottery—she may choose a hard shelf in a lonely store cupboard, or she may choose the foot of your bed. If she seems to be settling on a place that will not interfere unduly with your household routines, see that she has plenty of warm pieces of cloth or blanket that she can coax into a nest, and then do not disturb her unless you suspect that she is having difficulty. Normally, she will clean up after the birth without any help from you.

Dogs

Dogs make ideal pets. They enjoy human companionship, they love being taken for walks, they are not difficult to feed, and they are quite easily trained. They can be obtained, as the advertisements say, 'in a wide variety of shapes and sizes'. There are sporting dogs and cuddly dogs, swift dogs and sturdy dogs, dogs with long hair, dogs with short hair and dogs with barely any hair at all. Some dogs are more demonstrative than others, but once you have owned a dog and have earned its loyalty and affection you will feel strangely bereft if you ever have to live without one again. Most dog-lovers think that cats make very poor substitutes.

Fortunately for those who like them, dogs live for quite a long time, so you should choose your companion rather carefully. If you make a mistake (as, for example, if you buy a small puppy that appeals to you, and then find that it grows up into an active monster that is quite unsuitable for your home) you may have to put up with the consequences for several years—or part with your pet, which may not be easy. A visit to a dog show will help you to decide which breed you like best. Then you can study the advertisement columns in *Our Dogs* and *Dog World* to see what price you will have to pay for a puppy.

There are several advantages in having a thoroughbred dog. Not only will you know more or less what it is going to look like when it has finished growing, but you should be able to get quite a good idea of its temperament. Buying a mongrel, on the other hand, may be a bit of a gamble, especially if you have no chance of seeing its parents. You may get an absolute winner! Pedigree-bred or not, you should always take the healthiest and most active of a litter if you have a free choice.

It is usually safe to take a puppy away from its mother soon after it is eight weeks old, though it is best to be guided about this by the breeder. Check that the puppy has been completely weaned before you take it home, and check too that it has been treated for worms. The breeder will probably give you some advice about the kind of diet the puppy has been having and should continue to have, until it is comfortably settled in its new home.

During its first few nights after the move, a puppy may be given a temporary bed in quite a small box with high sides that will not allow it to escape. Give it some warm thick pieces of blanket to sleep on— and if it seems to want to go back to sleep during the daytime, do not disturb it. A puppy needs plenty of rest!

Later, when the puppy has grown rather larger, you will have to provide it with a more permanent bed. This should be large enough for the dog to lie in comfortably, it should be raised on legs at least three inches off the floor, it should have three sides to make it cosy, and it should be kept in a draught-free place. Put a piece of blanket for the dog to sleep on, and wash this out frequently, so that it never becomes smelly.

Before your dog has been in its new home for many days it should be house-trained or your life will become intolerable. Never smack a puppy when it misbehaves. When you see it sniffing round the corners of a room, or scratching at a door, you will have to take action, and quickly. If you take it out to the garden at frequent intervals— or to an outdoor sand-tray or earth-box if you haven't a garden—it will soon learn the purpose of the regular doses of fresh air.

Feeding a mature dog has become much easier since balanced canine foodstuffs have been packed and sold in tins. These make a good stand-by when you are unable to obtain suitable fresh meat, but you will want to give a young pup a rather more varied diet. He will need four meals a day at first, but the timetable can be gradually altered until by the time he is fully grown he will be able to manage with one main meal per day. This will be given, for preference, in the early evening. Some dog owners like to give an additional 'snack' of dry biscuits or meal during the morning. You will not go far wrong if you remember that meat forms a dog's natural diet, and it should preponderate, too, in the food a dog gets in a domesticated state. Besides chopped raw meat, your pet will appreciate porridge, milk, egg, chopped vegetables (not too much potato), brown bread (never white bread) and crumbled biscuits.

Don't give your dog titbits of any kind between its meals, or encourage anyone else to do so. If you feed it regularly, give it plenty of exercise, and let it have access to clean fresh water it should remain contented and healthy. There are a few infectious diseases that can affect dogs, of course, but a good vet., or your nearest animal clinic, will be glad to help you to protect your pet against these.

Dormice

Dormice are lovable little creatures. They spend a lot of their life in a drowsy state (country people sometimes refer to them as 'sleep mice') but when they are awake and active their red-brown coats, dark eyes and white underparts show to splendid advantage.

Unfortunately, dormice are not as common as they used to be, but you may occasionally find one in long grass or at the base of a hedge. Dormice from the Continent are sometimes offered for sale in pet shops. If you find a wild dormouse in winter and it appears to be dead put it in a moderately warm place for a short time and it will probably revive.

A good home for a dormouse can be made out of a large packing case. Preferably, this should be fitted with a glass front, so that the movements of the inmates can be studied. A small nesting chamber

Dormice can easily be distinguished by their very long tails

inside can be partly walled with glass, too. The cage should be properly ventilated, without the dormouse being subjected to draughts.

Dormice like the same kind of foods as squirrels—nuts, and more nuts, so that there is always a surplus that can be hoarded away for nutless days. They will also enjoy maize or corn, broken puppy biscuit, sunflower seed, and a little chopped fruit. Clean water should always be available.

Goats

Goats can be profitable pets, for they can produce large quantities of rich creamy milk every day, but don't let that induce you to invest in a goat unless you have plenty of space to keep it in, and plenty of time for looking after it. Goats can be as demanding as awkward children—and as exasperating!

Let's consider the question of space first. You *can* tether a goat with a rope or a chain so that its range is severely limited, but it is obviously better to let it wander freely in some kind of an enclosure if it is possible to do so. Unfortunately, a goat can, and will, escape from any territory that is inadequately contained, any boundary fence less than four feet high being easily negotiated by an active adult goat.

Next, you must provide some shelter, for goats do not like being left out in the rain. A small shed, with a door that can be fixed in an open or closed position as desired, is suitable. It can be fitted with a food tray a foot or so from the floor. Just above this, a rack can be arranged that will hold some sweet hay for the goat to nibble. On the floor scatter clean dry straw, dry bracken, or some other suitable bedding, but don't let this stay there too long before you change it. A goat that is given a chance to graze on growing grass, with hay to supplement this, will not need a lot of extra food. Bran, and crushed oats, or one of the proprietary goat feeds stocked by most animal shops and corn merchants will help in making up a balanced diet. Cabbage leaves and root vegetables will be enjoyed, but don't let a goat eat yew, privet or rhododendron leaves or the results may be disastrous.

Guinea pigs

Guinea pigs (or 'cavies') are delightful little creatures, and make splendid pets for the outhouse or garden. You can choose smooth-haired, self-coloured guinea pigs when you are starting a colony, because they are easy to look after, and keep spick and span without much grooming. Later, you can graduate to the long-haired varieties, and, perhaps, win prizes at shows with animals of your own breeding.

Perhaps it would be as well to make, or buy, a suitable home for your guinea pigs before you actually take possession of any.

A good draught-proof and rat-proof hutch can be made from a stout wooden packing case, all openings being covered with chicken wire. A hinged door or side will ensure that you can reach all parts of the hutch for cleaning. On the floor of the hutch put sawdust, and change it frequently so that it never has a chance to become foul. Dry, fresh straw and hay make splendid bedding.

As guinea pigs are so easy to keep and breed, it is more than likely that your colony will grow. If this happens, you can easily adapt an outside shed, or part of one, as a menagerie, arranging the hutches on shelves, or in stacks or tiers.

In dry weather in the summer, guinea pigs love to spend the daylight hours nibbling, in a leisurely fashion, on a lawn in the open air. To accommodate them under these conditions, make a low, portable pen by covering a light wooden framework with wire netting or chicken wire. Don't forget to keep part of the run shaded, for guinea pigs cannot stand strong direct sunlight for long. They need shelter, too, if it starts to rain.

Feeding guinea pigs is not difficult, because they will keep quite healthy on a basic diet of crushed oats and bran, varied occasionally with cabbage leaves, chopped root vegetables, clover, groundsel and plantain. In winter, keep all green foodstuffs in a warm place for a short time before you give them to your guinea pigs. Clean water should always be available.

Guinea pigs breed almost as prolifically as rabbits. If you decide to increase the numbers of your stock, you will be charmed by the youngsters when they first arrive, for they are born with their eyes open, and are not naked and helpless like so many young mammals.

Don't put two boars together in a cage, for they are almost certain to fight. You can put one boar with several sows though, and each of the females may well produce two, or even three, litters during the course of a year. There are usually two, three, or four young guinea pigs in a litter, and they arrive between nine and ten weeks after mating. When you suspect that one of your female guinea pigs is going to have a family, take her away from her adult companions and give her a quiet hutch of her own. Until they are big enough and strong enough to stand up for themselves, the young ones are liable to be trampled on.

Hedgehogs

Hedgehogs are an acquired taste. Because they are very rarely seen in broad daylight, except when they have been left on the roads as casualties of 'the Age of Speed', they are not often considered as possible pets. But no one who has found a hedgehog in the dusk in their garden could fail to be delighted by the quaint habits and amusing facial expressions of this well-protected quadruped.

Unfortunately, hedgehogs do not take kindly to captivity and you will not be able to keep one as a pet, and feel sure of its continued presence, unless your garden has a wall or fence all round it. Many gardeners like to have a resident hedgehog, or if not that, then a hedgehog which visits their garden frequently, for hedgehogs are hungry creatures and will keep down beetles, slugs and other pests in the course of their foraging.

If you do succeed in confining a hedgehog, or in coaxing one to stay, you will find that it will welcome a saucer full of bread and milk. If this is offered regularly, at a more or less fixed time, preferably around sundown, the hedgehog will become quite tame. Occasionally you can give it a little chopped raw meat or cooked liver as a change.

Normally, hedgehogs produce two litters a year, one in the spring and one in the late summer, so if you have a pair you may be able to welcome some of their delightful youngsters to the feeding saucer. The babies are born blind and with soft spines, but they soon become active and self-reliant.

A large garden will usually contain at least one border or wild place that is thick enough to give a hedgehog, or a hedgehog family, shelter and seclusion. If your garden is on the trim and tidy side you can provide a hutch, on the ground, to make up for the lack of natural cover. Put some dried leaves or straw in this as autumn approaches, for hedgehogs hibernate during cold weather and need some cosy spot in which they can sleep undisturbed.

Pigeons and doves

In the Middle Ages, many manor houses would have a roomy loft in or near the main building. In these cotes, colonies of pigeons or doves would live and grow fat, providing delicious meat for pies in the lean days of winter, and, in the summer, the gentle cooing and the soft swish of wings we associate with sunny gardens and ripening cornfields. You may not be tempted to keep birds of any kind to replenish your larder, but you can get a lot of pleasure from having two or three pairs of doves in an aviary, or some free-flying pigeons to centre round your home.

First, you will need a suitable building for your birds to live in, or to return to. If you want only a small number of free-flying birds, such as fantail pigeons, you can buy or make one of the small round cotes that look so attractive when they are mounted on poles in the middle of a lawn. Often, an empty barrel can be converted into a cote of this kind.

If you are going to keep a large flight for showing or racing you will need a dry shed, with a well-designed means of access to and from the outside world. The best way to find out about the advantages and drawbacks of the various types of loft is to mix with pigeon fanciers, so that you are invited to inspect and admire the quarters they have set up for their birds. Most experts will be pleased to help a beginner with advice.

Inside a loft there should be enough well-positioned perching places and some strong shelves on which you can put nesting boxes or pots (wooden trays, about eight inches square and two inches deep, will do splendidly). If you throw down some hay and straw on the floor of the loft as well as the usual layer of sawdust the birds will carry enough pieces up to line their nests as they want them.

It is always exciting to see one of your pigeons sitting on its

129

precious white eggs. When the young are hatched, you will be able to watch the parent birds feeding them with the regurgitated food known as 'pigeon's milk'.

The choice of birds for your loft is another matter on which you should seek expert advice, preferably from someone living in your immediate neighbourhood. There is no point in deciding to keep (say) Hooded Jacobins if there is a fancier living in the next street who will not only let you have some less exotic birds, but can tell you how to look after them as well.

All pet shops and corn merchants sell the foods on which pigeons and doves will flourish happily. Maize, wheat, maple peas and buckwheat form the staple diet, with weekly additions of hemp and canary seed to keep the birds in tip-top condition. Pigeons and doves need clean drinking water just as much as any other pets, and there are special preparations that can be added to water in a basin-bath to keep the birds' plumage free from tiny mites.

Rabbits

Rabbits can be kept in the very smallest garden—even a small shed will hold a hutch or two. They are gentle and attractive creatures, with no apparent urge to escape to a life in the wild. Their domesticated nature and their defencelessness may account at least in part for their great popularity.

Rabbits may be housed in any hutch that is roomy enough, well ventilated without being draughty (draughts may be quickly fatal), dry, even when the rain is pouring down, and having some part at least in shade when the sun is shining. Only an extraordinarily well-designed and well-carpentered hutch will be sufficiently weatherproof to stand out of doors all the year round. Usually, it is more satisfactory to place the hutch in some kind of shelter or lean-to.

On the floor of your hutch sprinkle sawdust with, perhaps, a little hay or straw, and if you have provided a separate sleeping compartment in the interior let this be fairly comfortably bedded with one of the latter.

Selecting your rabbits will not be easy, for there are so many varieties to choose from, each of which has its own specially attractive qualities. Among the most popular varieties are the Dutch, English, Himalayan and Rex rabbits in the medium sizes, the Belgian Hare and the Flemish Giant in the large sizes, and the tiny Netherland Dwarf as the smallest alternative of all. Don't invest in Angora rabbits unless you are prepared to spend a long time each day brushing their long, fine and exasperatingly easily tangled coats.

Rabbits are quite easy to feed, but they must be given meals at

A simple home-made rabbit hutch—note that the lid overlaps to protect the inside from rain

fairly frequent intervals so that food does not have to be left to lie about in their hutches to grow stale. They like hay, bran, crushed oats, chopped cabbage, carrot and swede, fresh grass, clover, groundsel and dandelion leaves. You can even give them bits of bread that you have baked hard in the oven, if you have some to use up. And rabbits—like all pets—need constant access to fresh water.

A pair of rabbits will breed readily—too readily, sometimes—and you may find the rearing of families quite the most interesting part of rabbit keeping. To make the doe's life as comfortable as possible when she is preparing to have a family take her away from the buck and, in fact, from all other rabbits, and give her a hutch of her own. This should have a secluded nesting box, if it is possible to provide one. She should be left alone and undisturbed for at least eight days after the arrival of her litter, though it is advisable to take just one quick peep at the nest when she is away from it if you suspect that one of the babies may have been born dead. Make sure you do not touch any of the live babies for the mother will destroy them if she detects human scent. Give her plenty of good, nourishing food while she is nursing her litter and she will bring her youngsters out for your inspection as soon as she thinks they are old enough to leave the nest.

Unfortunately, rabbits are rather susceptible to illnesses of various kinds, and you should seek the advice of a vet or some other qualified expert if one of your pets begins to show disturbing symptoms. You can have your rabbits immunized against myxomatosis, which is a terrible scourge. Most other rabbit diseases can be successfully treated with modern antibiotics. The important thing is to take action at once, before it is too late.

Top Common lizard   *Left* Adder   *Right* Grass snake

Reptiles and amphibians

Although they may not be at first sight as attractive as the smaller mammals described in these pages, many members of the reptile family make splendid pets. You can build a vivarium quite easily in your garden, but you may have to move the occupants indoors—or at least to the shelter of a greenhouse—during the winter months.

Frogs and toads can be reared from the spawn found in and near ponds and placid streams during March and early April. Give the tadpoles minute fragments of raw meat to eat, and some pieces of watercress, and you will enjoy watching their legs lengthen and their tails shrink as they grow out of their embryonic form. Your frogs will have a tendency to wander far afield once they have reached maturity; toads are much more placid, and may be quite

132

content to lead a comfortable and happy life in an ordinary suburban garden (there is a tame toad crawling round the author's feet, as he is writing these words!).

Lizards are great fun to watch, especially when they can be studied in their natural surroundings. Feed lizards, in a vivarium, on caterpillars, wood lice, earthworms, flies and other insects. In the winter you can keep them alive on mealworms, which you can breed specially by obtaining a 'culture' from a pet shop, keeping the worms on corn meal. Most lizards need a temperature of 65°-70° Fahrenheit, so you will have to provide some sort of heating if you intend to keep these pets through an ordinary winter.

Tortoises. A tortoise is probably the easiest pet of all to keep—as long as you can prevent it from wandering away on one of its

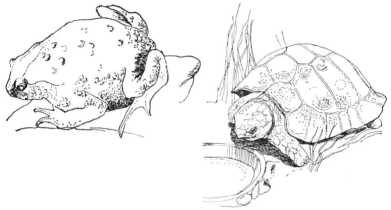

Toads and tortoises are slow-moving creatures, but they make charming pets

strange, slow, ruminative excursions. If you have a walled or fenced garden, the problem of straying will not arise. In an open garden, part can usually be boarded off. The barrier only needs to be a foot or so high, and this may also be arranged so that it discourages the tortoise from helping itself to precious seedlings and vegetables.

A tortoise's food needs no special preparation, as it will thrive on lettuce, spinach and cabbage leaves, as well as weeds such as clover, plantains and dandelions. Fresh water and some kind of waterproof shelter must always be available.

In the autumn a tortoise will lose its appetite, and if it is not watched it may try to make a winter retreat for itself by burrowing down into a soft flower bed, or by finding a hiding place in a deep bed of leaves. To give your pet a safe refuge for hibernation, put it in a box that contains hay, straw or dried leaves, and then put the box in a shed or outhouse where it will be reasonably well protected from frost until the following spring. It is not satisfactory to let a tortoise spend the winter in the living rooms of a house, as the variations of temperature make normal hibernation impossible and the poor creature will usually die.

Further reading

CHARLES TREVISICK, F.Z.S., *The Book of Pets* (Stanley Paul).
EDNA SIMMS, *Teach your Child about Pets* (Pearson).
FRANK MANOLSON, *D is for Dog* (Studio Vista).
ZDENEK VOGEL, *Reptiles and Amphibians* (Studio Vista).
IAN HARMAN, *Reptiles as Pets* (Blandford Press).

Photography

It would be interesting to know how many of the millions of photographs taken out of doors each year are intended to be anything more than a casual reminder of a fleeting moment—it would be even more interesting to know what proportion of them never 'come out' at all! With a little extra care and preparation even a holiday snapshot can be as pleasing to look at as a minor work of art. Let us review, briefly, the special equipment you will need, and the techniques you can employ, for successful outdoor photography.

Your camera. There are scores of attractive and reliable cameras on the market today at prices that range from a pound or two to many hundreds of pounds. Fortunately, there are some quite reasonably priced cameras that are perfectly suitable for outdoor work. Remember:

A simple box camera with a fixed-focus lens and a set shutter speed is relatively easy to use, but is rather limited in scope; it is quite unsuitable for close-ups, for example, and few subtle effects can be obtained with it.

A more expensive camera may have a lens with a focusing scale marked in feet or yards, or it may be fitted with a rangefinder, or with facilities for visual focusing on a ground glass screen. Any one of these will allow you to give sharp definition to any chosen part of your picture—which will invariably be the point of greatest interest.

A short-focus lens will give you greater depth of field than a long-focus lens—that is, the distance between the nearest point at which all objects are sharply defined and the furthest point at which all objects are sharply defined will be greater. This may be important if you intend to photograph many extensive landscapes.

A lens that has been specially 'bloomed' or coated reflects less light than an uncoated lens, and passes more light through to the film. This makes it slightly 'faster', or more sensitive.

If you want to take plenty of photographs without dipping into your pocket too deeply, a camera that takes 35 mm film may be just the type for you, as you can get thirty-six exposures on one length of film. Unfortunately, the photographs produced on these tiny negatives need a considerable amount of enlargement before they can be studied in any detail, and this often produces an unpleasant 'grainy' effect.

If you choose a camera that takes roll films of one of the standard sizes (eight, twelve or sixteen exposures to the spool) you will find that contact prints will be large enough for general reference, and that crisp enlargements can be made from specially good negatives.

The results you get from your camera will be in direct proportion to the thoroughness with which you master such operations as focusing, stopping down, and exposure calculating. But even if you become really proficient at the mechanics of picture-taking, your efforts may be wasted if you fail to

keep the camera clean
keep it out of strong sunshine
keep it in a sturdy case, where it is less likely to be damaged by knocks, rain, sea water, and other hazards.

Like all precision-built instruments, cameras demand their fair share of maintenance!

A lens hood. This is a small and inexpensive accessory that will vastly improve the quality of your outdoor photographs. It is intended to limit the number of stray light rays that can impinge on a lens when a photograph is being taken 'against the rules'—that is, with the main source of light at right angles to, or slightly in front of, the camera. As some of the most dramatic pictorial effects are produced by the rising and setting sun, you should be prepared to take photographs under the most testing conditions.

Filters. It is difficult to catch the full richness of the countryside or the dazzling contrasts of an April sky without at least one colour filter in your box of accessories.

Filters are usually made from pieces of coloured gelatine held between, and protected by, optically finished glass discs. Each should be held in a ring or rim that will fit snugly over your lens-holder. The function of a filter is to prevent light rays of a certain colour from getting through to the sensitive surface of a film or plate. This colour-sifting process can have two separate and equally valuable results.

It can adjust the hues and tints coming from a landscape so that a photograph made of that landscape corresponds more exactly to the image that the unaided eye receives, or thinks it receives.

It can help the camera to make a sharp image when a landscape is shrouded in a slight haze (yellow and orange filters are most often used for this).

As less light reaches the film or plate when a filter is being used, an increased exposure is called for. It is usually most practicable to open the stop.

A tripod. However steadily you may think you are holding your camera, you cannot be certain of getting as perfect definition as possible with every photograph you take outdoors unless you make use of a tripod. Tripods that fold away conveniently into a very small space can be obtained and are usually fitted with a tilting platform or a ball and socket head.

Getting 'life' into outdoor photographs. Quite often you will see a photograph taken out of doors that catches the attention because it has some particularly vivid quality, from which it is difficult to turn away. Every expert photographer will find his or her own favourite way of introducing a vital centre of interest into a picture. Strong shadows, groups of animated people, peasants in picturesque costumes, outdated pieces of farm equipment, animals and birds— all these have been used to add a little extra piquancy to landscapes that would otherwise have seemed a trifle empty or banal. Sometimes you can move such a feature into exactly the right part of your viewfinder simply by changing your own position.

Photographing landscapes. Your main aim when photographing a landscape should be to introduce as much 'distance' into the composition of your pictures as you possibly can. That does not mean that every photograph you take away from home must include a range of mountains, many miles away from your camera. Rather, it suggests that each photograph should contain one or two features that can very definitely be called 'foreground' features and some more that can take the viewer's eye back into the middle distance, and that there should be at least a hint of remoteness, to add spaciousness and perspective.

A landscape study with a colourless, cloudless sky generally tends to look a bit pale and anaemic. A yellow or orange filter may be just what is needed to give it the necessary contrasts.

Winter, when the deciduous trees are stripped of their shrouding and outworn foliage, offers splendid opportunities for landscape photography. Frost and snow-bound scenes can make especially attractive pictures. Use a yellow filter for snow, and counter glare by shortening exposures, or by 'stopping down'.

Photographing buildings. Many of the places you visit on your holidays will depend for their particular charm or interest on famous, historic or especially beautiful buildings. The photographs you take will be most graphic and effective if you can choose a time when the buildings are illuminated from one side. A 'dead front' light will tend to flatten them.

High buildings present some special problems. To get all of a many-storied building into one photograph you may have to stand so far back from it that you produce an empty and uninteresting foreground, or, alternatively, you may find yourself tilting your camera upwards. This may cause distortion, unless you happen to have a camera fitted with a special device known as a 'rising front'.

Specializing. There are many different kinds of subject for your camera outdoors, besides landscapes and buildings: boats and water, birds, animals, sporting events—all these are tantalizingly photogenic, but as each sets different problems of technique you cannot hope to do full justice to all of them without a certain amount of specialized study. There is rather a long list of books at the end of this chapter. You need not read them all, but among them you are sure to find one or two that will help you with your chosen lines of research.

Further reading

HOUSTON ROGERS, *Instructions to Young Photographers* (Museum Press).

ERIC J. HOSKING & CYRIL W. NEWBERRY, *The Art of Bird Photography* (Country Life).

M. LILLINGTON HALL, *Picture Making with Your Camera* (Newnes).

M. LILLINGTON HALL, *Colour Photography for the Amateur* (Newnes).

M. HASELGROVE, *Colour Photography* (Arco Publications).

J. D. MILLS, *How to Photograph Trains* (Fountain Press).

CARLTON WALLACE, *Photographing People* (Evans Bros).

ALEC PEARLMAN, *The Rollei Manual* (Fountain Press).

Ponds and pools

There is something very fascinating about a pond filled with still, clear water. If you are young enough, you will enjoy lying on your tummy and gazing down at the fish and insects and water snails and other small creatures that move around in its limpid depths; older people can get a lot of pleasure from seeing clouds, trees and flowers reflected in its glass-like surface. There are few people who will regard a pond, whether natural or artificial, with indifference. Do you know that you can add an attractive fishpool to your garden—and stock it—without an enormous amount of trouble and at very little expense?

First, you will have to decide how big the pool is to be, and at the same time you will want to decide on its position If you are lucky enough to have a stream running through your garden the problem of finding an adequate water supply will be solved. If you have to rely on the efficiency of your local Water Board don't site your pond too far from a tap! In either case, it should be where it will catch a certain amount of sunshine.

Next, you will have to decide how you are going to make the pond, you can dig out the bed and line it with concrete; you can use one of the already formed plastic pond beds sold nowadays, or you can buy one of the thick dark polythene sheets sold for lining small ornamental ponds at all shops that stock gardening equipment. Your decision will be affected by the size of the pond and the depth of your pocket.

Digging is, of course, hard and tiring work. You will be surprised how much earth you will have to remove to make a pond eight or nine feet long by three or four feet wide. Anything longer should not be embarked on without a lot of careful thought—you may not get nearly as much fun out of your pond if the fish and other inmates are a long way out in the middle, and virtually invisible.

You should give a certain amount of careful thought to the shape of your pond, too. An accurately constructed rectangular pond will not be nearly as interesting to look at as a pool that seems to have been formed by the natural conformation of the land. So, try to arrive at an outline that looks quite convincingly unplanned.

Using concrete. Let us assume that you are going to seal your pool with concrete.

To bed this down properly, you should first make a firm foundation for it by driving bricks, large stones and pieces of slate into the earth surface to be lined. If you have no other suitable materials use builders' hardcore or ashes.

Then get some planks if you think that they will be useful for keeping the concrete in place while it is setting. If you decide to make some extra deep pockets in the bed of the pool so that you can put water lilies or other aquatic plants in suitable anchorages later, you can use wooden boxes or small tea chests as 'formers' to establish the shape of the retaining walls, taking them away when the concrete has hardened.

To mix the concrete, take some of the best Portland cement (one part, by volume), clean sharp sand (two parts), and a clean coarse aggregate (three parts). The quality of this aggregate will determine the strength of the finished concrete, so try to find a mixture of shingle, ballast, broken stone and other hard materials that seems to be free from dust, unburned organic matter and clinkers. Ideally, the hard particles that make up the aggregate should be graded from $\frac{3}{16}$ in. to $\frac{3}{4}$ in. to ensure a really firm mix.

When you are satisfied with the ingredients, mix the cement, sand and aggregate thoroughly together in a dry state and then sprinkle water gradually over the mixture, working it and turning it with a spade until the resulting mash has a uniform colour and consistency, without being unduly sloppy.

There are no fixed rules about the thickness of concrete that should be applied to the floor and sides of a pond, but in most cases it is safe to assume that a coat 6 in. thick is quite adequate, a lesser thickness than this being apt to crack and cause leakage. Some pond-makers like to embed reinforcing materials such as coarse wire netting in the middle of a concrete layer.

Maturing a pond. Unfortunately, fresh concrete contains some alkaline substances that can be extremely harmful to plants and fish. Before you can stock a new concrete pond you will have to remove or neutralize these dangerous elements.

The best way of doing this may seem a bit long-winded, but it is sure in its effect—simply fill the pond with clean water, and then leave it to stand for several months. If, as is likely, you have made the pond in the summer or autumn, it will be ready to be drained, rinsed out and refilled in the following spring.

As a shorter alternative, fill the pond with water and then stir in enough permanganate of potash to make the water a dark wine-red. Empty the water away after a week or ten days, and then rinse the bed of the pool carefully before you refill it with fresh water.

Some craftsmen like to give the inner concrete surfaces of their garden pools a coat or two of paint, to seal them off, before they put any water in at all. When a light colour is chosen, the deeper recesses of the pool can be studied with greater ease.

Planting a pond. No fish or reptiles will live in your pond in a good state of health unless the water is shaded and oxygenated by a sufficient supply of suitable water plants. These will also provide food for the inmates, so get them well established before you turn your attention to the mobile stock.

Water lilies have a very ancient history and are among the most decorative of plants. Most varieties need to be planted in water between 1 ft 6 in. and 2 ft deep. The tubers must have some good rich compost around them—they can be packed down with loam, spiced with bone meal, on the bed of the pond before the water level is raised, or they can be lowered into position in boxes or baskets when the pond is full.

Most of the popular oxygenating plants you will be offered will increase in size and effectiveness very rapidly, especially if you introduce them into your pond in the spring or early summer, which is their time of maximum growth. Give them some ordinary loam—they will thrive quite happily enough without any manure or bone meal! Among the best plants to choose from are water crowfoot, which bears white, buttercup-like flowers in early spring; water milfoil, with fine, feathery foliage; the dark green willow moss and the pale green water starwort; and hornwort, although this tends to be rather brittle.

If you are introducing plants that you have gathered from wild sources, make sure that you wash them thoroughly before you plant them in your pond. If you don't, you may introduce algae (minute organisms that turn the water green) and other pests.

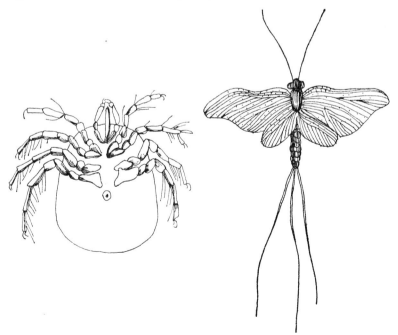

Left Water mite—a diminutive water spider *Right* Mayfly

Water snails make excellent scavengers and help to keep down algae. They can be found 'wild' in country ponds or bought from most pet shops. Ramshorns are to be preferred to fresh-water winkles because they do little or no damage to healthy growing water plants.

Fish. Don't introduce too many fish into your pond in your first flush of enthusiasm. If you overstock, the fish will soon lose condition and die.

Don't put fish together that are incompatible. Sticklebacks, for instance, will fight ferociously all other kinds of fish, and should have a pond to themselves; pike, perch, sunfish and catfish should be left out of a communal pond for the same reason. Roach are liable to develop an infectious fungus when they are kept in small ponds, and are also better passed by. And don't get any tench if you want the water in your pond to be crystal clear—they feed on debris, admittedly, but they keep on stirring up mud in the process!

Among the most satisfactory fish to keep in a garden pond are goldfish, which are both decorative and hardy and will quite often produce young ones in June or July; shubunkins, which are not unlike goldfish, except that they are a little slimmer and appear to have no scales; carp and golden orfe, and the amusing black moor, which, however, has to be brought in to an indoor aquarium during the winter months.

Ice. If ice forms on your pond in severe weather, don't try to smash it, or you will kill all your fish with concussion. They will probably survive if the pond freezes completely, but when a cold spell seems likely to continue you can admit oxygen by pouring hot water, from a kettle, on the same spot each day.

Further reading
FRANCES PERRY, *The Garden Pool* (W. H. and L. Collingridge).

Pony trekking

Some hobbies have been popular for many generations. Others, previously almost unknown, have aroused widespread interest quite suddenly when a few far-sighted people have realized their possibilities. Among the latter is pony-trekking, which now provides exciting and invigorating holidays for hundreds of fortunate adventurers every year. It is a hobby that can take you to many wonderful places, in the mountains perhaps, or on remote moorlands, that you might not otherwise ever have a chance to visit.

Don't be put off pony-trekking by the knowledge that you have never ridden a horse of any kind before. All recognized trekking establishments keep carefully selected ponies that can be guaranteed to give even an absolute beginner a comfortable ride. Some of these 'patent safetys' need little or no guidance from the tyro they are carrying. There is an instructor in charge of the trek—that is all the ponies need to know.

Planning. As pony-trekking is most enjoyable in reasonably good weather, it is usually carried on in spring, summer and early autumn. Most trekking establishments close down and give their ponies a well-earned rest during the winter.

During the riding season it is hard to find a vacant place at any of the best-known centres and advance booking is now the general rule. Here are the addresses of some organizations that may help you to get fixed up:

The Central Council of Physical Recreation,
6 Bedford Square, London WC1.
The Ponies of Britain Club,
Brookside Farm, Ascot, Berkshire.
The Workers' Travel Association,
Eccleston Court, Gillingham Street, London SW1.
The Holiday Fellowship,
Fellowship House, 142 Great North Way, Hendon, London NW4.
The Co-operative Holidays Association,
Birch Heys, Cromwell Range, Manchester 14.
The Youth Hostels Association,
Trevelyan House, St Albans, Herts.
The Scottish Youth Hostels Association,
7 Bruntsfield Crescent, Edinburgh 10.
The Welsh Pony Trekking Association,
Wyeside, Builth Wells, Breconshire.
The Scottish Council of Physical Recreation,
4 Queensferry Street, Edinburgh 2.

Many hotels in the West Country, Wales, the Lake District and

Scotland have close links with some local riding stables, and guests at them can go pony-trekking at special all-in rates. The best hold Ponies of Britain Club certificates, or are approved by the Scottish Council of Physical Recreation.

Clothing. You will not need to bother about Royal Enclosure standards of clothing when you are away on a pony-trekking holiday, but you will be well advised to choose clothes of a more or less traditional type that have been proved to be suitable for riding.

Riding breeches or jodhpurs are comfortable and will allow you to move your limbs freely, but you can wear an old pair of drill or corduroy trousers instead if you have never bought any clothes specially for riding and if you need to cut down expense. A tweed jacket with large pockets will be warm and comfortable unless the weather is very wet and cold. Under rigorous conditions you may need a short overcoat or macintosh and a thick pullover as well.

It is important to be well shod when you are pony-trekking, as you may have to dismount and lead your pony through all kinds of rocky, marshy and even waterlogged places. That is one reason why a complete change of clothing (to be stored at your trekking head-quarters) is almost essential. The second reason is purely social: fond as you may become of your pony, you won't want to spend every single evening of your holidays hanging around the stables in the clothes you have been wearing all day!

How a pony-trekking holiday is organized. Most pony-trekking centres take guests by the week. Trekkers arrive on Saturday, ready

for an early start on Sunday morning. Usually, packed lunches are taken each day, and it is delightful to picnic in some remote and beautiful spot while the ponies have their midday rest, a chance to graze, and, perhaps, their own few handfuls of feed.

Shortly after you arrive at your trekking centre the organizer will ask you how much riding (if any) you have done before, and according to your experience you will be allotted a suitable pony, which, normally, will be your partner for the duration of your stay. You will probably become quite attached to it by the end of that time!

You will also be instructed in some of the simple operations that have to be carried out if you are to enjoy your holiday to the full, without being a nuisance to other people. These will probably include:

Managing your own 'tack'. You will be expected to fetch your own tack (or equipment) from the store or saddle room, and to return it there in good condition at the end of the day's trek.

Feeding, watering and grooming. None of these tasks will prove difficult, as you will be doing them under the guidance of a patient instructor.

Saddling up. You will be shown how to saddle and bridle your pony so that it is perfectly comfortable during the trek (and so that you are, too). If the lengths of your leathers are not properly adjusted to suit you, personally, you may have a most unpleasant ride. If the pony's girths are not tight enough, the saddle may slip. You will be treating these and several other points as routine matters by the third or fourth day of your stay at the centre.

Mounting and dismounting. Stand on the near side of the pony (that is, facing the pony's tail, with your left shoulder near the pony's left shoulder) and the instructor will show you how to place your left foot in the stirrup, how to steady yourself by holding the back of the saddle, and how to swing your right leg over to the further side of the pony, so that you are facing the right way. Dismounting is even easier, as long as you remember to take *both* feet out of the

stirrups before you lean forward and swing yourself off the pony's back.

Trekking manners. Everyone taking part in a pony trek should observe certain conventions of behaviour so that the passage of the ponies through the countryside adds to the delights of the landscape, instead of spoiling its peace and its charm. Try to observe the following rules:

Keep in single file, in your appointed place in the queue. The organizer or instructor almost certainly had a very good reason for putting you there. Let your pony go at the pace set by the leader. Don't lag behind or your steed may suddenly feel lonely, with disastrous results.

Shut all gates, if you ever find yourself on the last pony in a file. The others should wait until you have done this before they move on.

Dismount without arguments when the person in charge of your trek suggests that you should. You will impress nobody by 'acting independent', but you may cause quite a lot of people quite a lot of hilarity if, through foolhardiness, you tumble off. You should go pony trekking to provide amusement for yourself, not for others!

Further reading

J. KERR HUNTER, *Pony Trekking for All* (Thomas Nelson).
GLENDA SPOONER, *Instructions in Ponymastership* (Museum Press).

Rambling

There is a great difference between walking for pleasure, and walking because one has no other means of transport. If you choose rambling as a recreation, you won't notice the miles you cover—you will have so much to look at, and to think about, as you make your way towards your destination. Don't be a haphazard pedestrian, though. To be completely enjoyable, rambling calls for as much careful planning as any other outdoor hobby.

In country like this you can ramble for days

Clothing. There is no point in setting out for a long walk in the wrong kind of clothes. If you wear clothes that you like, and in which you are really comfortable, you will feel relaxed and contented even at the end of a tiring day. Clothes should never be chosen just because they happen to be fashionable. A garment that is too tight in any particular place may flatter the figure, but it can cause intolerable discomfort on a long walk if it starts to chafe and chap the flesh.

There are other possible causes of discomfort you can guard against. Nettles, brambles, thorns and thistles may prove a nuisance when you are walking over very rough ground. Strong sunshine can cause sunburn and blistering. So don't leave your legs and arms exposed for many hours unless you have been spending a lot of time out of doors and are reasonably well hardened to fresh air hazards. It is very tempting to rush into shorts and other brief garments on the first day of a holiday but you may regret your rashness later if you are over-hasty.

Be careful, too, not to be over-optimistic about the weather. A sudden shower may be quite an exhilarating experience when you are out walking in open country, but wet clothes are uncomfortable to move about in, and can cause chills. Excellent waterproof macintoshes and capes can be obtained from most shops that sell camping equipment, and are designed to fold away into a very small space when not in use. Beware of the cheapest, lightest, plastic macintoshes, as these may be ripped to pieces by the gusts of high wind you must expect to encounter in exposed places.

There is one more point to remember when you are choosing clothes for rambling: a lot of the interest you get from your walks will come from the animals, birds and other wild creatures you may come across. Obviously, you won't see many of the shyest creatures, which are so exciting to encounter, if you are wearing brightly coloured clothes. All true naturalists try to make themselves as unobtrusive as possible, so opt for muted grey, green and brown garments if you have any choice in the matter.

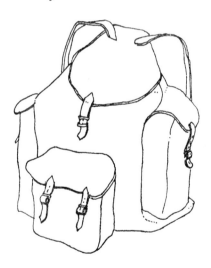

Rucksacks. When you go out for any really long walks, you may find a rucksack useful for carrying food, spare clothing, and other essentials. If you go on a rambling holiday, you won't be able to do without one.

When you are shopping for a rucksack (and when you are filling it) remember that every ounce you carry on your back is liable to feel like half a ton at the end of a long day's tramp. Therefore, you will find it advisable to invest in a modern, scientifically designed rucksack which has a tubular steel framework. This may cost you a little more than one of the floppy haversacks that are suspended from webbing shoulder straps, but you will appreciate the extra comfort it affords, for it will spread the load you are carrying over the whole of the upper part of your back. Splendid rucksacks can be bought from:

Messrs Thomas Black and Sons Ltd,
The Industrial Estate, Port Glasgow, Scotland
and Messrs Bukta Ltd,
Brinksway, Stockport, Cheshire

and from the local retailers who stock their products. The Scout Shop, at 25 Buckingham Palace Road, London SW1, is a good place to visit if you are anywhere near.

There is no point in buying a light rucksack if you are going to load it with a lot of unnecessary luggage. Take a piece of paper and a pencil when you are planning a ramble and make a list of the bare essentials you will need on the way. If you are going in company, begin by sharing the basic load equally between every one of the walkers, then if anyone else wishes to take any extra personal belongings, the additional weight can be his own responsibility.

Give a little thought to the order in which you pack your rucksack. Anything you are likely to want fairly often, such as a map, should go near the top where you can get at it easily.

Walking shoes or boots. A sound, comfortable pair of shoes or boots is essential. If your walk is to be thoroughly enjoyable, you should not be conscious of your feet! Thin plimsolls may be very comfortable for running about in on a school playground, but they are not suitable for long rambles in mountainous country. Really

strong shoes or boots, fitted with nails, will take a lot more punishment without causing any discomfort to the wearer. Excellent footwear for rambling can be obtained from Messrs William Timpson Ltd, Great Ducie Street, Manchester 3.

Don't try going for a long walk in new boots or shoes. All footwear —even the best—needs to be broken in gently. If you are going walking where conditions are likely to be damp, you will be most comfortable if your shoes or boots have been recently waterproofed. Give them a generous dressing with Dubbin or neats' foot oil from time to time, being especially careful to do this just before you put them into storage, between rambling holidays.

Maps. A lot of the pleasure you get from walking will be lost if you have to spend any part of your time wondering where you are, or how you are going to reach your destination. It is almost essential, therefore, to have a good map with you, and to refer to it frequently.

Ordnance Survey maps will give you any guidance you need, wherever you are walking in Great Britain. The maps drawn to the scale 1 in. to 1 mile are probably most suitable for ramblers—anything drawn to a smaller scale being a little less informative, anything larger tending to be unwieldy.

Messrs Bartholomew and Geographia Ltd also produce maps that can be highly recommended for ramblers. For a little extra outlay, you can buy maps with linen backs that will stand up to strong winds better than the ordinary unreinforced paper variety.

To help you to orientate a map correctly (and to find your bearings if a thick mist descends on you suddenly, as is liable to happen in mountainous country) you may decide to carry a pocket compass. If by any chance you find yourself without a compass, you can find out where you are in various ways, and these will be described a little later in this chapter under the heading 'Getting Lost'.

First aid and foot comfort. However jealously you may be guarding the space in your rucksack or pockets, you should always manage to find room for any equipment or materials you may need to help you to cope with small mishaps, or to ensure foot comfort. First Aid is dealt with in more detail in the chapter on Camping, but here are some brief notes about the special problems that may confront you when you are on a rambling holiday:

Blisters. They are the bugbear of all long distance walkers. To prevent them, try dabbing your feet with methylated spirit a day or two before you set off on your travels, and then take some with you so that you can repeat the process at intervals. Take some talcum powder or boracic powder for dusting your feet and some adhesive dressings to protect any part of your skin that becomes blistered and sore.

Cuts and scratches. A small bottle of antiseptic and a little surgical cotton wool should be included in your kit, for dealing with these.
Sprains. Trained medical help should be sought if there is any chance that a rambling mishap may have serious consequences. A slight sprain should be treated with a cold water compress, followed by rest.

Over the hills and far away. Once you are ready to start rambling, you will probably be keen to cover a great many miles as soon as you possibly can, but do be sensible about the first walks you take—don't let them be too long, or too exhausting! It is only too easy to be tempted to go a mile or two further than you had originally planned, and the extra distance may make you so tired and sore that you won't feel like walking at all on the following day. It is better to cover four or five miles only on each of the first two or three days of a holiday, increasing your range as you become fully physically fit.

There is another reason why it is better to walk in a leisurely fashion at the beginning of a rambling holiday: your powers of observation (as well as your muscles) will probably need to be brought into tiptop trim. As you wander in a relaxed manner through the countryside you will have a chance to notice all the small signs that can tell you so much about the wild life around you, if you are able to interpret them. There are several ways in which you can acquire the knowledge necessary for enjoying a ramble to the full—by reading books, by attending lectures, and by keeping your own nature log, to name only three. You may not be lucky enough to be able to travel through the countryside in the company of a trained naturalist, but seize the opportunity if you can, for such a walk can be an unforgettable experience.

Rights of way. As long as you keep to the roads and footpaths shown on a large scale Ordnance Survey map, and as long as you conduct yourself with normal decorum you are not likely to be accused of being a nuisance, or of trespassing on private property. Once you branch off into open country, you will be on less sure ground. Here are some notes that may help to keep you out of trouble.

Enclosed land. Nobody may walk on any person's property without permission unless there is a recognized 'right of way'. When you are not sure if a right of way exists, you should get in touch with the owner if you possibly can, and ask for his consent. You will not often be refused permission.
Common land. Occasionally you will find yourself walking across 'common land'—that is, uncultivated ground which does not belong to one specific owner. It is quite wrong to suppose that ramblers can do exactly as they like on common land—as often as not, these tracts are jealously guarded, and rash intruders who try

to camp there or light fires or otherwise make nuisances of themselves are quickly corrected. Don't be afraid to ask for information from the police in the locality. They may be able to direct you to alternative camping sites if the place you have your eye on is out of bounds.

Getting lost. Every year a number of ramblers are involved in mishaps that are the direct results of carelessness or lack of foresight. Make sure that you are not one of the unfortunate people who get lost, or injured, or worse, through misplaced enthusiasm.

You are not likely to lose your bearings for long if you keep to the roads and lanes that are marked on your map for most lowland districts nowadays are well supplied with signposts. When you are walking in mountainous country, or on open moorland, you may find it rather more difficult to reach your destination, especially if a mist suddenly descends, as can so easily happen when one is more than a few hundred feet above sea level. Here are some notes that may help you to ramble as safely and surely as an experienced explorer.

Compass bearings. To use a map to find out where you are, you must be able to 'orientate' it—that is, you must be able to move it round so that the 'north' of the map agrees with compass north. If you are carrying a compass, the job is easy. If you are without one, you will have to use your wits—or your pocket watch or wrist watch. Put the watch on a flat surface and move it round until the hour hand points in the direction of the sun. To find south you will have to draw an imaginary line that is exactly halfway between the hour hand of the watch at that moment and its position at twelve o'clock. The imaginary line will point due south. But don't forget that the clocks may have been put forward by an hour, if you are doing this in high summer. You will have to allow for that!

Visibility, nil. If the sun is hidden, as, for example, when you have been taken unawares by a thick most, you will not be able to use a watch or your powers of observation to establish your bearings. Don't let the fact that you are lost make you flustered. If there is no necessity for you to move, stay where you are until you can see a greater distance. If you must strike out into the unknown, try to find some running water—even a tiny trickle will join up with others eventually and will lead you down to lower ground and, finally, to a valley.

The main thing to avoid when you are lost in thick mist or fog is aimless, circuitous walking, which can exhaust you without getting you out of trouble. If you fail to find running water, and if you have no idea where you are going, try to find shelter behind a wall, a tree or a boulder and use that as your base. Call for help as loudly as you can at regular intervals. This will attract the attention of anyone in the immediate vicinity who may be able to help you, and it will announce your whereabouts to anyone who is actually trying to find you.

Youth hostels. The problem of 'where to stay' when you are on a walking tour may be solved quite easily if you belong to the Youth Hostels Association (National Office: Trevelyan House, St Albans, Herts). There are more than 250 friendly hostels in England and Wales, and a YHA membership card will admit you to similar hostels in Scotland, Ireland and over thirty countries abroad. The hostels, which are intended to enable all people to explore the countryside at low cost, are of great variety; if you join, you will be able to stay at farmhouses, water mills, cottages, mansions, specially built hostels, and even, at St Briavels in the Lower Wye Valley, in a picturesque medieval castle.

The accommodation at some youth hostels is excitingly austere, but all the hostels provide adequate facilities for an overnight stay, including dormitories, washing places, a common room and a members' kitchen. These kitchens are fully equipped with cooking points, utensils, crockery and cutlery. They are used by many members not only to keep down their expenses, but because they enjoy the fun of a 'cook-it-yourself' holiday. Other hostellers prefer to purchase meals cooked by the wardens in charge of the hostels. This service is available at most hostels, and the meals are substantial, suited to the large appetites created by outdoor activities! If you like meeting people—and, perhaps, making new friends—you will find plenty of opportunities on a youth hostelling holiday.

Further reading
GUY R. WILLIAMS, *Use Your Legs!* (Chapman and Hall).

Maps
JOHN BARTHOLOMEW & SON LTD, 12 DUNCAN STREET, EDINBURGH 9.
GEOGRAPHIA LTD, 68 FLEET STREET, LONDON EC4.

Running for pleasure

This chapter has been entitled 'Running for Pleasure' instead of just 'Running', because there are certain steps you can take to make this, one of the simplest and most straightforward of activities, a thoroughly enjoyable hobby instead of an occasionally necessary labour.

Training. The first step, and the most important, is to get into training. It is quite impossible to run successfully, or even comfortably, unless you have taken some pains to get every part of your body into really tip-top condition. Experts recommend:

A moderate diet. That is, plenty of nourishing food, eaten at regular meal times (and not between), and chosen to provide a satisfying and well-balanced diet. Greasy foods should be avoided, and so should unusually rich, spicy or exotic dishes. If you are going to do any competitive running, don't eat anything just before the race. Some coaches insist on a gap of three or four hours between the last meal and the start of the race.

A carefully regulated training programme. It is impossible to lay down one schedule that will suit everyone. As a general principle it is safe to say that a moderate amount of exercise and training, taken regularly, will be more effective than over-exertion at widely spaced intervals. You can increase distances and pace gradually when your body starts to conform to the demands you are making on it.

Sufficient rest and sleep. All athletes in training need regular and adequate hours of sleep so that their bodies can recuperate properly from their abnormal exertions.

Temperate habits. It is easy to say 'Don't smoke! Don't drink alcohol! Don't eat a lot of sweets!' and so on, but we each tend to indulge ourselves in different ways, and a prohibition that may be a sacrifice for one person will be a matter of complete indifference for another. Fortunately, the importance of getting into training is usually so compulsive, once we start, that we don't mind cutting out all forms of dissipation.

A correct mental attitude. This is almost as important as a well-regulated physical condition. If you train sensibly your confidence in yourself and your ability to fight fatigue will increase in direct proportion to your physical condition.

Shoes. Fortunately, very little equipment is required for running—a pair of suitable shoes being the most expensive item on the list. For cross-country running, special leather-topped shoes are sold that have small rubber studs for better gripping. These are excellent in muddy and frosty conditions. Many advanced long distance runners keep a pair of spiked cross-country shoes as well. In this kind of shoe there are usually six widely-spaced spikes on the underside of the sole. The heel is made of rubber, and is not fitted with spikes.

Clothing. Any clothing you wear for running must be light, absorbent and comfortable. Most athletes choose wool, cotton or rayon T-shirts for races and practice sessions, with regulation track shorts of any suitable lightweight material. Socks must fit snugly, so that the risk of blisters is minimised. A thick woollen track suit is a useful thing to have, but is liable to be rather expensive.

Clubs. In most districts there are athletics clubs and teams of harriers. You will find it useful to join such a club if you become really interested in running. Watch the columns of your local papers for reports and announcements, or write for information to the Amateur Athletic Association, 26 Park Crescent, London W1.

Further reading
PETER HILDRETH, *Athletics* (Arco Handybooks).
DON CANHAM, *Cross-country Running* (Herbert Jenkins).

Rush basketry

Rush basketry is a delightful hobby for those who are reasonably clever with their fingers. The baskets you can weave will make splendid presents, and your pastime may even prove quite profitable as Christmas approaches.

The rush harvest. Rush basketry need cost you nothing at all. You will find suitable rushes for weaving along most slow-moving rivers and canals, and around ponds and lakes. They reach their best height and condition just after midsummer, so they should be gathered during July and August, when drying conditions are good.

Lay your rushes to dry on a clean, flat surface, spacing them out as widely as possible so that the warm summer air can reach every leaf. If any moisture is left in them, they will probably deteriorate quickly and become mildewy. Properly dried rushes have delightfully natural colours, ranging from fresh yellows and yellow-greens to the warm brown tone of a harvest loaf.

Preparing rushes for weaving. Dry rushes are not very easy to weave. Put your rushes under wet cloths or sacking to make them more flexible for twenty-four hours at least before you use them.

Weaving. For your first exercises in rush basketry you will probably find it easiest to use a temporary foundation. A cardboard carton or a wooden box of a suitable size will make a splendid former. Fix the rushes in position on the former with pins, drawing pins or tacks.

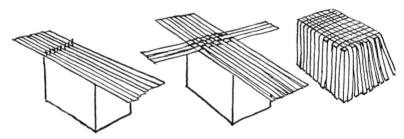

First, set up the base by turning the former upside down, so that the base is uppermost.

Then cut enough lengths of rush to stretch along the length of the base and up each side to the rim of the basket. It is difficult to estimate how many of these lengths will be needed, unless one knows the width of the rushes being used. Cut the lengths from the butt end (the wide end) of the rushes, and, as all rushes tend to taper, arrange the blades alternately, with the wide end of one rush at one end of the box, the wide end of the next at the other, and so on. Keep the rushes in their correct relative positions by inserting a row of pins or

156

tacks along one edge of the base. Don't pin both ends, or you will find it impossible to weave the base.

Next cut enough lengths of rush to weave the base. These should be long enough to stretch across the base at right angles to the rushes already on it, and to fold up to the rim on each of the sides. Again it is difficult to say how many will be needed, but if you intend to weave any kind of pattern into the sides of the basket you should try to use an odd number, so that the middle rush will form the 'centre line' of the design.

Weave each of these weft rushes through the stakes already pinned to the base, using a straightforward 'over and under' weave, and packing each rush as close to its neighbour as possible. Once again, it is best to use the rushes in alternate directions to take up the taper.

When the weaving of the base is completed, bend the stakes across each of the sides and ends of the box, and pin or tack them in place near the rim.

Upsetting. This is the name given to a specially firm weave used to establish the shape of the sides of a basket, and the next two or three rows you weave should, therefore, be straightforward 'pairing' packed down as tightly on the side stakes as possible.

Add new rushes, when needed, by putting the end of the new rush against the last few inches of the old rush, weaving them in together as one piece. In this way weaving becomes continuous, spare ends of rush being easily 'trimmed' off when the basket has been completed.

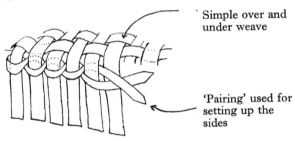

Simple over and
under weave

'Pairing' used for
setting up the
sides

Weaving the sides. After you have set up the side stakes you can use a simple over and under weave again for weaving the sides. When you have woven two or three baskets, you may decide to add a little variety to your work by weaving in ornamental patterns—letting one rush pass over two others before it passes behind a third is a simple example of the methods used to obtain a noticeable difference of texture. If you set up the sides with two rows of pairing, finish them off with two rows of pairing to make them symmetrical before beginning the border.

Weaving a border. The simplest edging for a light basket like this is known as a 'three rod plain border' and you will see how to carry it

157

out if you look at the illustration on this page. The flatness of your rushes, however, will not allow you to make a tidily woven border unless you give each rush one complete twist before each movement or stroke. If you do this correctly, working the ends into the weave when you have completed the round, a firm and thoroughly satisfactory border should result.

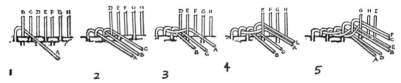

A three-rod plain border that can be used for completing a rush basket

Handles. A basket without a handle is not much use to anyone! A handle can be plaited quite easily and then sewn into position with strong cord or twine. Alternatively, you can work some rushes through the pairing immediately under the border and then you can bind them round to make a comfortable grip.

Plaited rush baskets. If you have managed to prepare a good supply of rushes, you may like to try plaiting a number of them together so that you can make some really substantial and useful articles for the household, such as log baskets, and rush mats.

To plait rushes, tie six, nine or even twelve strands together with strong raffia or twine and fasten the tied end to something steady such as a post or door handle. You may find it more convenient to carry out this work in a garden or yard, plaiting in a straight line from the starting point until there is a continuous rope of rush many feet in length.

Towards the end of each rush, lay the end of a new one inside the last few inches of the old and plait them in together. Experience will show you some of the finer points that you will have to watch if you are to turn out really first class work. The three cords, for example, of which each plait is made up should be kept as even as possible. To do this you may have to increase or decrease the number of rushes which make up each of the cords. Plaited basketry, too, executed by a real expert will have all the 'ends' emerging on the same side of the plait, so that one side is quite free from untidy oddments, and can be used for the outside of the finished work. But these are refinements that can be safely neglected during the earliest stages.

When you have made a plait long enough for whatever you are planning to make, bind the ends securely with raffia or strong twine and trim off any projecting pieces of rush as close to the plait as possible.

Sewing the plait. For sewing plaited rushes into shape, you will need strong fingers, and one of the special curved needles you can obtain from Dryad Handicrafts, 22 Bloomsbury Street, London WC1 (or Northgates, Leeds) or from any shop that sells materials for craftworkers. Thread the needle with raffia or strong twine.

Begin by sewing the base or floor of the basket. A straightforward coil will make a basket with a circular floor. If you stitch a loop 10 in. or 12 in. long before you start to sew the plaiting round it, you will produce an oval-floored basket.

Each row of plaiting has to be stitched securely to the preceding row if the basket is to be strong, and the stitches should be made on the inside, rather than the outside, if the finished basket is to look tidy. You will find that the base of your basket is easier to keep flat if you hold it down on a table—or some other firm working surface while you sew it.

When the base is as large as you want it to be, bring the plait to the top of the outside row, instead of to the side of it and stitch down through the two plaits, so starting the wall of the basket. Work two rows of stitches round the first ring of the wall, laying the second row diagonally over the first for extra strength.

Then sew successive rows of plaiting together, in an upward spiral, until the walls reach the height you have planned for them to be.

To finish the walls neatly, reduce the size of the last length of plait gradually by removing the plaited rushes one by one until the plait is thin enough to be worked unobtrusively to the inside of the preceding row. There it should be sewed and bound into place.

A handle for a plaited rush basket. Take a length of plait as long as you want the handle to be, bind it tightly for an inch or two at each end, and then sew the ends into position on either side of the basket. If you want to make these joints extremely neat, leave an inch or two of unbound plaiting to project beyond the binding. You can fray this out after you have sewn the handle into position.

Further reading
M. Roffey & C. S. Cross, *Rush Work* (Pitman).

Left and mid. Starting bases for round and rectangular baskets *Right* Finished plaited rush basket

Sightseeing

Are you the kind of person who enjoys a conducted tour of a place of historical interest? Or do you prefer to walk round by yourself, finding your own way and noticing the things that it pleases you to observe, without wondering if they are mentioned in the guide books or not? Human beings can be divided, for fun, into two distinct categories—those who can stand being lectured at, and those who can't. If you are one of the independent ones, the pages that follow may help you to get some extra pleasure and interest from your solitary excursions.

Equipment. It may seem a laughable proposition, that anyone should need any special equipment for sightseeing, but you will get a lot more pleasure from your visits to notable places if you take a powerful pocket torch with you, and a pair of binoculars.

The torch will help you to examine many features that would otherwise be hidden in a cast shadow, or shrouded in general gloom—as, for instance, the wonderfully comic carvings to be found under the miserere seats in old monastic buildings. There are some splendid examples to be seen in Exeter Cathedral.

The binoculars will enable you to enjoy fascinating architectural details that are too high up to be studied with the naked eye (the carved stone water spouts on many cathedrals and churches are often fantastic caricatures of persons known to, and sometimes disliked by, the mason). Even a pocket mirror may be useful when you want to look at the intricate bosses and graining in a medieval ceiling.

Preparation for sightseeing. He sees most, who knows what to look for. That is an ancient adage, but it is still perfectly true. An expert will stop in his tour of an ecclesiastical building and study (say) an almost imperceptible hole in a thick stone pillar. The layman will pass by it without a glance, not realizing, as the expert does, that it is a 'squint', a specially contrived visual aid that enabled a worshipper to keep an eye trained on the altar, ready for the elevation of the Host at the climax of the principal service. That is only one example of the many interesting features you may notice in an old edifice if you have trained yourself, by reading books and by asking questions, to be really observant.

Looking at churches. When you visit any town or village you have never been to before, it is a good idea to look round the church, for it will almost certainly be one of the most ancient buildings in the locality, and even if it is of comparatively recent construction it may well be standing on ground that has been reserved for rites and ceremonies since pre-Christian times—perhaps for many thousands of years.

There are five things to look for before you go into a church:

The churchyard gate. This may have a little roof over it, which was intended to shelter the priest while he was conducting the first part of a burial service. Look carefully, there is an outside chance that you may be seeing one of the rare medieval lich-gates, or a copy of one.

The yew trees. These may be extremely ancient. Some yew trees growing in sanctified ground may have been planted, originally, in pre-Christian days.

Crosses. Many Christian churches were built on the sites of pagan shrines. This was a deliberate policy on the part of the Church authorities, as they found that people were still meeting in those places for what the Christians considered improper purposes. The first act of the new users of a site would be the erection of a large stone or wooden cross as a proclamation of faith. Some of these crosses were splendidly carved, and of great beauty, but many of them were destroyed during the Reformation (sixteenth century), only the base and, sometimes, the shaft being left to show us the site of the earliest Christian graves in the locality.

A sundial. Until Greenwich Mean Time was generally adopted during the nineteenth century, each district would have its own local time, which varied from place to place according to the meridian. To establish local time there would usually be (in the oldest churches) a sundial on the south wall of the church, and in more recent buildings a free-standing sundial somewhere in the churchyard. Look for a sundial (or the traces of one) in each church you visit, noticing particularly the division of the day into tides (prime, none, terce, sext and vespers) instead of hours in some of the earliest dials. You will enjoy the elaborate inscriptions on the later and more accessible sundials, too. Some of these enabled the parishioners to estimate the time in remote parts of the world, as well as in the immediate vicinity.

Tombstones. These bear silent testimony to the history of a town or village, and they are not always as gloomy as their initial purpose would inevitably seem to make them. What could be more delightful than this inscription from the little church at Hilton, in Dorset? There, the lawful minister, John Antram, was deprived of his living during the years 1646 to 1660. At the Restoration, his living was given back to him, and when he died he was buried in the grave of his lawful predecessor, one Robert Roche. The double grave is distinguished by this epitaph:

THE BODYS HERE OF TWO DIVINES EMBRACE
BOTH OF WHICH WERE ONCE THE PASTORS OF THIS PLACE,
AND IF THEIR CORPS EACH OTHER SEEM TO GREET
WHAT WILL THEY DO WHEN SOUL AND BODY MEET?

161

You may find some equally amusing sentiments that have never been recorded before in the rarely-trodden corners of almost any country churchyard, so take a notebook with you, in which to copy them down.

Fonts. When you enter a cathedral or church, look first at the font, for it may be the most venerable feature there. Before the Reformation, christening water was actually kept in the stone basin of a font, instead of being taken there just before the service as it is nowadays (sometimes, in a Thermos flask). Naturally, it was a constant temptation to unscrupulous people, who wanted to purloin the precious fluid for use in spells, love potions and home-made patent medicines. So wooden covers with locks were fitted to most fonts, and these

Top left and middle In the 11th century the decoration of capitals of pillars became elaborate *Right* Norman pillar showing typical chevron markings *Bottom left* Norman font with characteristic rounded arch pattern

remained in use until the Reformers derided the importance that had been attached to the ritual element in baptism. Then they were removed, and you can still see in many fonts the holes and recesses from which the fittings were torn roughly away.

The interior of a church may be completely representative of one architectural style, or it may be a mixture of styles. If you would like to be able to give an approximate 'date' to any part of a church, you can study this section. Here, very briefly, are the principal stages into which many experts like to subdivide the development of church architecture:

Saxon (to AD 1060, approximately). Few Saxon churches are left now. You can usually recognize Saxon work by the arrangement (alternately) of long upright and short horizontal stones at the corners of the masonry. The short bulbous pillars that can be seen in the rudimentary windows are also characteristic.

Norman (AD 1060 to AD 1200, approximately). Real Norman buildings have two unmistakable features: semi-circular arches over doors and windows, and the zig-zag or 'chevron' patterns with which so many of the stone surfaces are decorated. The great Norman abbeys at St Albans and Tewkesbury and the cathedral at Durham are among the finest ecclesiastical buildings in Britain.

Early English (AD 1200 to AD 1271, approximately). The first fine flowering of the Gothic movement, which followed the introduction of the pointed arch. Look for high 'lancet' windows, and the carved motif known as 'dog-tooth ornament'.

Decorated (AD 1272 to AD 1349, approximately). A later and more exotic development of the Gothic style. In the first half of the fourteenth century, craftsmen became extremely proficient at carving intricate forms, with naturalistic foliage and fruit and the distinctive 'ball flower' ornament predominating.

Perpendicular (AD 1350 to AD 1530, approximately). The spacious and sedate style evolved at Gloucester, in which some of the finest English churches, chapels, shrines and colleges were constructed during two eventful centuries. Splendid examples of perpendicular

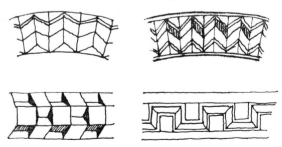

Top Typical Norman chevron patterning *Bottom* The more rectangular look of early English carving

tracery and delicate fan vaulting can be seen and studied at Oxford and Cambridge.

Classical. With the introduction of classical forms, the great age of Gothic churchbuilding was over. Churches designed and erected in the seventeenth and eighteenth centuries are relatively uncommon, but invariably elegant.

Gothic Revival. An experienced sightseer can usually tell whether he, or she, is inspecting a 'real' Gothic church or a more recent building designed 'in the Gothic manner'. Many churches were restored, some in the process completely spoiled, during the nineteenth century.

Before you leave a church, see if it has any of these interesting features:

A rood screen. The chancel, used by the clergy, and the nave, used by the congregation, would sometimes be separated by a richly carved wooden screen. This would be surmounted by a cross or 'rood' (hence its name) and at Christmas and other festivals would be most beautifully illuminated with candles. Some rood screens included small galleries that were intended to accommodate the parish musicians.

A piscina. This is a small recess in a wall, usually near the altar or near the site of a vanished side-chapel. In the recess there would be (and often still is) a shallow basin with a drain leading out to the churchyard. At the end of the communion service, the scourings of the sacred vessels would be poured away down this drain into the earth of the churchyard, which, being itself consecrated, would not cause defilement.

Dog tongs. Used for removing intruding pets in the days when a bite could easily produce a fatal illness.

Bassoons, pibcorns, serpents and other ancient musical instruments. These are often preserved in a place of safety, having well earned their honourable retirement.

Looking at castles. Castles, being deliberately made as strong as possible, have a tendency to last if they are not deliberately destroyed. By looking round ancient strongholds we can get a good idea, even in this mechanised era, of the surroundings in which heroes and warriors lived and died during the age of chivalry.

Not all the castles you see will be immediately recognizable as such. When the Normans advanced into Britain after the Battle of Hastings (1066) they had to erect a number of temporary strongholds that would allow them to retain their grip on the countryside until they had had a chance to construct more ambitious fortifications. These early Norman castles invariably consist of a mound or 'motte' and a 'bailey' or enclosure. Both the motte and the bailey would be protected with hastily dug ditches, soil ramparts, and timber stockades.

164

The timber stockades have all rotted or have been burned away, but you can still see the earthworks, even if, as in many cases, they have been rampantly overgrown.

Later Norman castles were at the time almost impregnable, their square or round 'keeps' having walls up to twenty feet thick. In a keep there would be all the workshops, armouries and storehouses that could possibly be needed in the course of a long siege. These would be arranged, usually, on several floors which were connected by spiral staircases. Norman keeps in an excellent state of preservation can be seen at Rochester and Dover. The White Tower in the Tower of London is another very famous example.

King Edward I was one of the most successful of all castle builders, the massive strongholds he created when he was trying to subjugate the Welsh being, even today, in an age of enormous buildings, extremely impressive. Conway, Caernarvon, Beaumaris, Harlech—a visit to any one of these castles can hardly fail to be an exciting experience, and you will enjoy it even more if you know a little about the science of fortification. Here are a few of the things you ought to look for if you are walking round a castle built in the twelfth or thirteenth centuries:

The barbican. This is a structure or outwork designed to give extra protection to the gateway. It may be a raised approach, flanked by a precipice, as at Conway, or a stone screen pierced with loopholes, as at Beaumaris. Almost any external addition that can be used as a man trap will, in fact, qualify for the name.

The moat. This may still be present, though it may well have been drained. Try to imagine what the castle would look like with water around it, making the walls reflected in it seem doubly forbidding. And see if the sluices are left—and how they were guarded.

The gatehouse. This imposing structure will usually reflect the fearsomeness and obduracy of its designer, for it was intended to be awe-inspiring. It may have a statue, a heraldic device, or a motto over the entrance way, which will be worth observing. So, too, will be the aptly named *meurtrières*, or 'murder-holes', immediately overhead.

A drawbridge. This, essential if there were a moat, may be still in existence. If it has crumbled away, look for traces of the drawbridge fittings in the gatehouse walls. Many drawbridges were counter-poised, and you may be able to see the recesses in the masonry made for the controlling framework.

A portcullis. This was a grid-like gate, made of wood and iron, that was raised and lowered by means of a winch in the interior of the gatehouse, or by the use of counterpoise weights. Few portcullises survive, but you can see in several castles the *chase* or slot through which the portcullis descended, and the grooves that controlled its sides.

Towers. At least three kinds of tower may be found in medieval castles—mural towers, used for defending the curtain walling; household towers, used for accommodating distinguished persons and officials and their entourages, as well as for defence; and towers planned for some special purpose—as kitchens, perhaps, or armouries. The round mural towers usually found in Edwardian castles are sometimes known as 'drum' towers.

Curtain walls. These are the defensive walls that fill the gaps between the towers or between the angles of castles. Along the crest of a curtain wall you will normally find the :

Battlements. These usually consisted of three parts—the *alure*, or footwalk; the protecting *parapet*; and an open work gallery or *machicolation.* The parapet would probably be *crenellated*, or made with gaps or 'crenels' at regular intervals, so that soldiers manning the battlement could take cover behind the high stone *merlons* when they were not looking out, or taking aim. Through the vertical gaps in the machicolation they could drop missiles or hot fluids on any attackers who approached the base-courses of the wall.

The hall. The Great Hall was the pivotal point of a castle's life. Councils of war were held there, and trials, and, in moments of relaxation, banquets and theatricals or masques. Many castle halls can now only be traced through the footings of the walls.

The dungeons. This word is generally applied to a cellar or basement room that was used as a prison, and it should not be confused with a 'donjon' as this properly means the whole keep. There is a fearsome pit-like dungeon at Berkeley castle in Gloucestershire, into which prisoners were peremptorily thrown.

Looking at great houses. Fortunately for us, many of the finest houses to be seen now belong to the National Trust, and some of the others that are still in private hands can be viewed on certain days in the year. Domestic architecture is a very wide field of study, and people who enjoy looking at timber-framed Tudor mansions with inglenook fireplaces and diamond-paned windows may get no pleasure at all from the subtle simplicity of a Georgian façade. Whatever your taste, there are certain features to look for when you are visiting any house of special interest. The first of these is, obviously, the lodge.

Lodges and gatehouses. These usually give the sightseer some idea of the style and scale of the residence beyond. Ornamental gate piers, heraldic devices, gatekeepers' dwellings and magnificent wrought iron gates are often combined to make architectural compositions of great charm and elegance.

Structure. If you keep asking yourself how the house you are examining was built, you will be more likely to notice the small structural details that give so much information to the trained eye.

Even the size of the bricks used may help you to determine the probable date of a building. For example, some thirteenth-century bricks found at Little Wenham, Hull, were each 9 in. × 4½ in., by 2 in., while the bricks used in some eighteenth-century houses in Rodney Street, Liverpool, are 9½ in. × 4½ in. × 3 in. These, and many other interesting facts may be found in Nathaniel Lloyd's *A History of English Brickwork*. Other information books are listed at the end of this section.

Dummy windows. During the reign of King William III (1689-1702), the Government decided to levy a tax on windows. This was particularly difficult to avoid, as the buildings being designed at that time were in the classical taste, with lights arranged in a balanced, symmetrical way. So all but the very wealthiest people would have a window or two bricked up, to reduce their payments, and often they would have the infilling brickwork painted to look as if there were in fact still glass there. It may amuse you to look out for examples of these expedients.

Follies. It may amuse you to look out for follies, too. These are high towers, erected at the whim of sportive landowners, and serve no useful purpose except (usually) to provide a magnificent view. Near Lydeard St Lawrence in Somerset you can visit Winter's Folly which was built about 1790, possibly as a gamekeeper's dwelling. There is a late eighteenth-century Tower Folly near Tawstock in Devon, and, at Faringdon in Berkshire, Lord Berners' Folly which was built as recently as 1935.

Hillside figures. Several hillsides in Britain are given added interest by the outsize figures or animals that can be discerned, even from long distances, on their slopes. The origins of many of these hillside markings are wrapped in mystery, but among those thought to be the most ancient are:

The Man of Cerne, near Cerne Abbas, Dorset. (A naked giant, brandishing a club).
The Long Man of Wilmington, near Wilmington, Sussex. (A man with a wand in each hand.)
The Uffington White Horse, near Uffington, Berkshire.
The Bledlow Cross, at Bledlow, Buckinghamshire.
The Whiteleaf Cross, near Princes Risborough, Buckinghamshire.

Horses that are definitely of more recent origin than that at Uffington can be seen at Thirsk and Northwaite in Yorkshire, Tysoe in Warwickshire, and Westbury and several other places in Wiltshire. There is a hillside lion, that dates from 1933, near Whipsnade Zoo.

Further reading
JOHN HARVEY, *The English Cathedral* (Batsford).

VICTOR BONHAM CARTER, *Exploring Parish Churches* (Routledge and Kegan Paul).

J. CHARLES COX, *The Parish Churches of England* (Batsford).

JOHN BETJEMAN (Ed.), *Collins Guide to English Parish Churches* (Collins).

JOHN BETJEMAN (Ed.), *English Churches* (Studio Vista).

MORRIS MARPLES, *White Horses and Other Hill Figures* (Country Life).

A NEEDHAM & J. LITTLEJOHNS, *How to Study an Old Church* (Batsford).

W. DOUGLAS SIMPSON, *Exploring Castles* (Routledge and Kegal Paul).

REGINALD TURNOR, *The Smaller English House* (Batsford).

See also section on Archaeology.

Sketching

Wherever you go, when you are out of doors, you will see things that are exciting to look at, and to remember. Your attention may be caught by a group of fine horses under a tree, or by a black and white cottage reflected in a placid mill stream, or by a pair of swans with their cygnets, or by some bronzed figures in a harvest field in the hot August sun. If you want to make quick visual records of all the scenes that appeal to you, you may find it worthwhile to take photography seriously. If you like drawing, on the other hand, you can get a lot of extra enjoyment by carrying a sketchbook with you on your outings and holidays. You do not have to be a fully trained artist, or even a moderately proficient one, to have a lot of fun with a pencil or pen.

Buying a sketchbook. Sketchbooks of many kinds, and at a wide range of prices, can be bought at all shops that stock artists' materials. For your purposes, you may find that one of the thick sketchbooks made specially for art students is most suitable. These contain many dozens of leaves of thin Bank paper, and this, being reasonably cheap, makes sketching a comparatively economical hobby. You will be able to draw much more freely—and, incidentally, much more successfully—if you are working on a surface that you can scrap with a clear conscience when anything goes wrong.

Don't think, though, that you need to go out to buy a sketchbook before you can start drawing out of doors. Many artists like to carry a small pocket folder about with them, slipping into this any loose pieces of paper that may be of a convenient size and surface. You can make a useful folder of this kind from two rectangular pieces of hardboard by placing them together, edge to edge. Glue a strip of cloth over the division between them, add some side flaps made from thin card to stop the contents slipping out, and you will have a replenishable pocket sketchbook that you can take with you wherever you go.

Pencils. Pencils suitable for sketching are marketed in a number of different grades, according to their hardness or softness.

Hard pencils, such as 4 H or 6 H, are splendid for exact architectural studies, but you cannot use them to produce really dark tones, so the sketches you make with them may tend to look rather thin and lifeless.

Soft pencils, such as 4 B or 6 B, will produce rich dark tones, but they are not really suitable for sketches where a lot of fine lines are required.

Pencils from the medium grades such as H, HB and B are ideal for most general purposes. If you want to be really well equipped, you can take one of each of these with you, together with one of the rich, velvety pencils made specially for sketching, such as the 'Black Prince' or the 'Black Beauty'.

Pen and ink sketching. Many people enjoy sketching with pens and ink, because they find that this technique compels them to make up their minds quickly and to act decisively. With a pen you have to put down boldly and directly what you see, instead of stroking the paper timorously, as you can all too easily with a pencil!

Almost any fountain pen with a fine strong nib will do for outdoor sketching. Take a small bottle of ink with you, too—it is frustrating to find your pen dry when you are ready to start work. If you can include a sable brush in your outfit, you can add subtle tones to an ink drawing by reinforcing the ink lines with carefully-laid washes of clean water. The water will dilute or dissolve the ink, and the resulting tints will give the drawing the same sparkle and vitality as we enjoy in an attractive landscape on a showery day.

Charcoal. The charcoal sold for use by artists is usually made from fine sticks of vine or willow. You will find it invaluable for producing rich grey-black tones with extreme speed, but it tends to be easily smudged, and all drawings made with charcoal should, therefore, be sprayed with fixative at the earliest possible opportunity.

Fixative can be bought from any supplier of artists' materials, and so too can a spray diffuser, by means of which you can blow a fine film of the liquid over the surface of your work. If you run out of fixative when you are far from any source of supply, you may be able to make some for yourself like this: shred some white shellac into a bottle, cover it with methylated spirit, and shake until the shellac has dissolved.

Sketching out of doors can be most enjoyable if you equip yourself with some toned paper (such as grey sugar paper), charcoal (for the dark tones) and white chalks (for the light tones and high lights).

Crayons. These are sometimes useful for adding a suggestion of colour to a sketch, but if they are used too freely they will produce a shiny, waxy surface which is not particularly pleasant.

Pastels. These compressed, chalky colours are made up in short sticks. They are easy to carry, but unfortunately it is not easy to produce a wide range of shades and tints by mixing them, so you may have to include quite a large number of different pastels in your outfit if you wish to produce sketches of any subtlety. Like charcoal, pastels tend to be easily smudged, so a sketch made with them should be sprayed lightly with fixative as soon as it has reached its final state.

Proportion. As soon as you start sketching, you will be faced with a difficult problem: how are you going to make the image you are producing on your paper correspond as exactly as possible to the subject you are trying to represent?

To be able to sketch successfully, you will have to be able to judge proportions accurately. You cannot hope to reproduce a house (or a tree, or a mountain) convincingly on paper unless you can relate correctly its height, its width, and its depth or thickness.

Let us suppose that you have settled down to sketch an unspoiled Norman church in a remote district. The tower of the church is (say) X feet high, and it is Y feet wide at the top. If you make an error of judgement and represent it as if it is X feet high but Z feet wide at the top, your drawing will never look exactly like that particular church, though it may be, by accident, pleasantly reminiscent of another church, somewhere else!

Holding your pencil or pen at arm's length may help you to assess proportions accurately. If you hold your arm out very stiff and straight and if you make sure that the pencil or pen is as nearly as possible at right angles to it you can use the end of your thumb as a marker —that is, you can cut off on the shank of the pencil or pen the apparent length of any part of the scene in front of you. Then you will be able to compare this length with any other length, simply by moving your arm or by turning your wrist. The right time to take a measurement of this kind is when you are starting a drawing, not when you are working on the final details. Then, it may be too late!

Light and shade. As you become increasingly proficient at sketching, you will become more and more aware of the importance of

light and shade. Without light you would not be able to see any of the three-dimensional shapes in front of you, nor could you hope to be able to reproduce them by drawing or painting on flat, two-dimensional surfaces. Sooner or later, you will cease to be content with the bare outlines which you will almost certainly have used for your earliest sketches, and you will start to use 'tone', as artists call shading of various kinds, to add strength and an appearance of solidity to your work.

At first you may not find it easy to build up a dark tone smoothly and speedily with a pencil, but a little practice on a clean sheet of waste paper will show you how you may most satisfactorily impose one set of lines over another so that the lines tend to disappear, forming a dark, even, grey tone without gaps or black furrows.

Try, first, drawing two sets of parallel lines that cross each other at right angles. Then draw two more sets of parallel lines that cross each other more acutely—at an angle, say, of 15° or 20°. You will probably notice that the second set is more readily accepted by the eye as an even tone than the first. This method, which is known by artists as 'cross-hatching', produces a more pleasing effect than 'stumping', or smudging, charcoal or pencil lines with rolled-up blotting paper, which is sometimes recommended as a means of applying dark tones to a drawing.

Generally speaking, all the people and objects you draw will be lightest where their surfaces face the source of light, and darkest

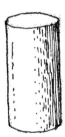

Basic forms to look for when sketching: the cube and the cylinder

where their surfaces are turned away from it. You will not be able to carry the shading of a sketch very far, therefore, without deciding where the light is coming from and, if there is more than one source of light, which is the strongest or principal source. Immediately you start a sketch look for the cast shadows. These are the dark shadows thrown on the ground plane by the forms that are standing, or resting, on it and they will tell you all you need to know about the 'lighting scheme'.

Let us see, next, how you can use an elementary knowledge of light and shade when you are sketching out of doors.

You will be able to demonstrate in your drawing the difference between forms that are composed of flat planes, such as the church tower already mentioned, and forms that are composed of curved surfaces, such as the round drum towers of an Edwardian castle. The former may have flat areas of tone, each surface having a separate value—dark, medium or light. The latter will be affected by the gradual change from light to dark known as 'graduation'.

You will be able to show the difference, in the same way, between forms that resemble cones and forms that resemble pyramids. The tones on a flower pot, for example, may well change gradually from light to dark, but there will probably be a distinct 'arris' or change of plane where each pair of flat surfaces in a gabled roof adjoin. Each arris is shown, in a shaded drawing, by a distinct and sudden change of tone.

Cast shadows are important, because they can help you to establish the size and the shape of the forms that are throwing them. A tall man, for example, will probably throw a longer shadow under normal conditions of sunlight than a short man standing just behind him. That may seem obvious, but have you realized that an artist can show that one of the men is an inch or two off the ground—by leaving a small gap between the soles of the man's feet and the shadow he is throwing? You will only see strong cast shadows, with hard, distinct edges, when the sun is shining brightly, or under the influence of an artificial spotlight. On a cloudy day you may find it difficult to see cast shadows at all, unless you look for them specially.

Drawing buildings. You don't have to know a lot about architecture to enjoy drawing buildings. They are as still as anything you are likely to encounter in a normal landscape, and so you will be able to take your time over them, making studies that are correct in proportion, and attractively shaded.

Here are two hints that will help you to make your sketches of buildings completely convincing:

Uprights. Every normal building or group of buildings contains a number of lines that are as nearly vertical as an artisan's plumb-line can make them. Plot these lines on your sketching pad, and

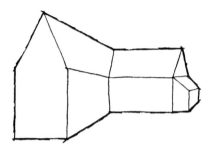

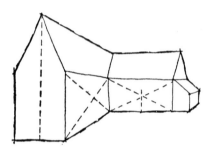

When you are sketching buildings get the basic shapes right first (top), then you will find it easy to place the details correctly you will have a helpful scaffolding on which to construct the rest of your drawing.

Details. Don't put any doors or windows or other architectural details into your drawing until you are sure that you have assessed the basic forms of the building or buildings correctly. Work from the major shapes to the minor shapes, and your drawing is not likely to go seriously astray.

Drawing trees. The best time to draw trees is during the winter, if you can bear to sketch out of doors then! In the summer, the boughs and branches of a healthy deciduous tree are shrouded by foliage, and it is difficult to trace the natural forms of growth which give that tree its peculiar character.

Whatever the season, any drawing you make of a tree will be most successful if you concentrate first on the trunk and the main branches. To nourish themselves, all trees have to draw mineral salts in solution out of the earth, and then they have to expose those salts to the action of as much fresh air and sunlight as possible. Each kind of tree does this in a different way and if you can observe the route followed by the sap as it travels from the ground to the outmost leaves you will be well on the way to capturing the 'personality' and the charm of that particular species.

As the branches of a tree grow further from the trunk they tend to decrease in thickness until they are at last quite light and insubstantial. It is important to notice this natural taper when you are drawing every part of a tree, and to give it its full value. If you don't, your sketch will tend to look clumsy and graceless.

A tree covered with leaves in summer may seem very difficult to draw, because the soft forms of the foliage are not as clearly defined as the more substantial forms of rocks, walls and buildings. You can make the task a lot easier by imagining that the tree has been carved out of some solid material such as wood or soap. This requires some mental effort but it will help you to distribute the areas of light and shade most convincingly. You can add a texture that suggests leafiness afterwards, when the solidity of the tree has been safely established.

Drawing people. Figures are often used to add interest, liveliness, and a suggestion of scale to landscape sketches, but you may well find people extremely difficult to draw, because they will not keep still for very long unless they are bribed or forcibly persuaded! After you have had some practice, however, you will find an increasing number of figures making their appearance in your sketch book. Stand for a few minutes in a crowded market place and you will see plenty of people you would like to record—men with gnarled, weatherbeaten faces, women who remind you of the monsters in Hogarth's paintings, children with innocent, mischievous, sly and

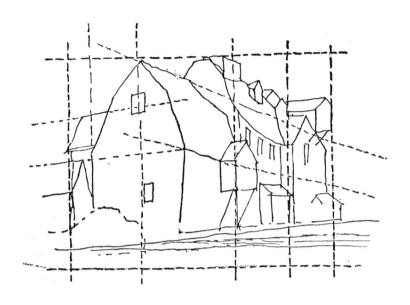

In this drawing of a mill the basic shape has first been sketched and the dotted lines in the top illustration act as a guide to proportion and perspective

downright wicked expressions—all these should be observed and their facial characteristics should be noted down before they move out of sight, or before the visual memory of them fades.

At first you may find it hard to draw figures which are moving, or are in a pose that indicates some temporarily arrested activity. You may be defeated by the difficulty of drawing someone diving, for example, or kneeling down to take a mole or some other small animal out of a trap. When you are faced with this problem, try drawing the trunk or torso of your 'model' first, simplifying the shape

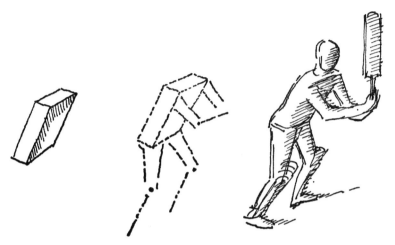

A simple shape like a matchbox may help you to sketch a figure in a 'difficult' pose

so that it resembles an enlarged matchbox. This will help you to establish the angle at which the body is poised. It will also help you to represent it as a solid form. Subtleties can come afterwards, and so can the head and limbs. You will find it much easier to draw these convincingly if you have first constructed a correctly proportioned body to which you can relate them.

Drawing animals. You can use, as a drawing aid, a simple shape like a rectangular box if you want to draw an animal, too. The proportions of the box will vary according to the type of animal you wish to portray, but with a little practice you will soon become quite proficient at making the horses you draw seem really like horses, and the cows like cows. If you can spend some time sketching in a market-place, a zoo, or even (though this may not be quite so exciting) in a museum, you will soon learn to ignore the silky sheen of an animal's hide or the soft texture of its fur, forgetting these until you have traced as much as you can of its tense, logical bone structure. Direct

177

your thoughts towards the anatomy of the animals you are studying and your drawings will have real vitality and truth.

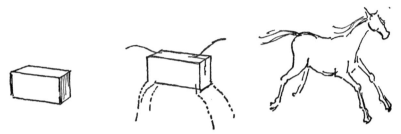

Similarly you can start to draw an animal by 'laying in' a rectangular box

Perspective. Linear perspective, tonal perspective and colour perspective present many puzzling problems with which an artist has to grapple if he wishes to represent a three-dimensional subject (that is, a real part of the visible world) on a two-dimensional surface (that is, on paper or canvas). You can produce some splendid sketches without going into these problems too deeply. Consider the parallel sides of a road, canal or river, for instance. If you are standing where these lines recede from you towards the horizon, you will probably notice that they appear to move closer to each other until they meet, finally, at a point known to artists as the 'vanishing point'. This vanishing point should be located and marked plainly on the paper on which you are sketching, as a guide. If the road, canal or river changes direction to right or to left, a new vanishing point will come into being, on the right side or the left side of the original vanishing point, according to the alteration of course. When a road starts to go uphill, a new vanishing point will be needed— *above* the horizon. When a road starts to go downhill, its parallel sides will appear to converge on a point *below* the horizon. These elementary rules are easy to remember, and you will find outdoor sketching much more enjoyable if you bear them in mind.

Aerial perspective or 'tonal' perspective is quite easy to understand, too. All you have to remember is the neutralizing effect of distance, thus:

Foreground. The darkest shadows and the most brilliant highlights can only be found in the immediate foreground of a landscape, where everything is close to the artist's eye.
Middle distance. In the middle distance, both shadows and highlights are muted—the darkest shadows are comparatively pale, and the brightest lights are comparatively dull.
Background. When you are drawing things that you can see only dimly, in the farthest distance, the range of tones you can see is

limited indeed. Try drawing a hill a mile away from you, and see if you can make it look a mile away from you, just by the delicacy with which you handle your pencil or pen.

You will not be greatly concerned with colour perspective if you are sketching with a pencil or pen. When you are using water colours

Note how the perspective lines meet at eye level

or oil colours you will find that your work gains interest and vitality if you use your strongest colours in the foreground and if you keep for the distance only the coolest, softest 'pastel shades'—tints of purple and blue and the palest greys. Colour is neutralized by distance, as well as tone—that's a fact that it pays a painter to remember!

Further reading
GUY R. WILLIAMS, *Sketching in Pencil* (Pitman).
GUY R. WILLIAMS, *Drawing and Sketching* (Museum Press).
MAURICE WILSON, *Drawing Animals* (Studio Vista).
FAITH JAQUES, *Drawing in Pen and Ink* (Studio Vista).
ROBERT FAWCETT, *On the Art of Drawing* (Studio Vista).

Tracking

The people who enjoy life most are often those who have learned to use their senses to their fullest capacity. They seem to see more, and hear more, than duller mortals with the same number of eyes and ears! People who spend most of their working life out of doors in the country—gamekeepers, for instance—seem to develop an extra sense: they can pick up multitudes of 'messages' left by animals, reptiles, insects and birds that would escape the notice of even the most observant town dweller. You, too, can get more fun from the hours you spend in the open air if you learn to study the movements of the interesting creatures that are most often unseen and unheard. 'Tracking,' we may call this hobby, though the study of paw- and claw-marks in the ground may only form a part of it.

Animals and their homes. Many wild animals are nocturnal in their habits—that is to say, you will stand no chance of seeing them in their natural surroundings unless you are prepared to stay out very late in the evening. However, it is worth taking a pair of binoculars with you in case you see something before dusk. Then, you are more likely to be able to study them if you know where they live. Here are some of their 'Home' signs:

The fox lives in an 'earth', which may be like a deep, wide-mouthed rabbit burrow, a hollowed-out interstice in the roots of a tree, or a narrow cleft in some (to humans) inaccessible rocks. If an earth is still lived in, you may see fresh tracks where the fox has squeezed itself down at the entrance, and you will almost certainly catch a whiff of the animals' unmistakably pungent smell.

Sometimes, your attention may be drawn to an earth that a fox has taken over from a fox or some other occupant—the previous owner's bedding will have been carried to the ground outside by the new tenant, and left there.

The badger lives in a 'sett', which may be rather like a fox-earth, but is certain to be better upholstered and very much cleaner. Some badger setts are like a maze of tunnels, with dozens of entrances. You may see, near a sett, a tree that has been used as a 'scratching post' by badgers.

The otter lives in a 'holt' near the water's edge. You will be a super-naturalist if you can locate a holt unaided, for the entrance as often as not will only be approachable by an underwater route.

You will stand more chance of seeing a fox, a badger or an otter—or any other shy wild animal—if you learn to keep so still that you become part of the landscape. It will help if you wear clothes that are neutral in tone and colour. Take up your position near an earth or sett at least an hour before sunset, in a 'hide' of branches if you can possibly arrange one quietly. And don't forget that an animal may be warned of your approach by its keen sense of smell while you are still hundreds of yards away. A clever tracker always keeps downwind of his—or her—objective.

Tracks and trails. Many wild animals are creatures of habit—a fox may emerge from its earth at exactly the same time each evening, and set off on its travels by a favourite path: each of the rabbits from one warren may have its usual place for negotiating a hedge or a piece of damp ground, and be loath to alter it. The observant countryman sees the parted twigs or the disturbed blades of grass and knows that he is by one of these carefully chosen routes—he is drawing on lore accumulated by generations of poachers and gin-setters.

Soft ground and mud in the country are usually well worth careful study. You may find the journey-marks of a heron, an otter, a rat or a water hen near a river or a lake, the long divided slot of the fallow deer in lonely woodlands, the cat-like pad-prints of a marauding fox near a farmyard, and the tiny traces of voles, shrews and field mice almost anywhere. Carry a sketch-book around with you and record any of these 'signatures' you may come across, whether you are able to identify them without further reference or not. The authorities at the Natural History Museum at South Kensington will help you if you come across the tracks of any creature which may be really rare.

Plaster casting. To record more permanently any interesting tracks

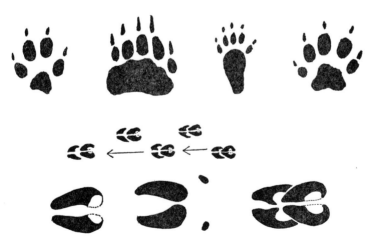

These are some of the distinctive tracks you may enjoy looking for when you are out in the country *Top, left to right* Fox, badger, squirrel, otter *Bottom* 'Slots' of deer

181

you may find, you will need some plaster of paris, a bowl, or some other vessel for mixing it in, and a strip of flexible card or plastic that you can use as a containing wall.

First, choose the most distinct impression—if there are a number of marks—and clear away from it any loose leaves, lumps of mud, twigs, small stones or other bits of debris. Then set up the containing wall in a circle around it, using paper clips or gummed strip to retain it at a convenient diameter. Bank up sand or earth around the lower part of the outside so that the plaster will have no chance to escape.

When you have had a little experience, you will be able to gauge exactly how much water and plaster will be needed to make each disc so that it finishes about ¾ in. thick. Put your estimated amount of water in your mixing bowl, sprinkle dry plaster into it until a small cone appears on the surface and remains dry, and then agitate the mixture rapidly until there are no air bubbles or dry lumps in it. Then pour it carefully into the mould. If you are likely to want to hang the plaque up on a wall or screen, tuck the ends of a string or tape loop into the upper surface of the plaster.

Within a quarter of an hour the plaster should have set quite hard, and may be removed from the mould. Wrap the plaque carefully in several sheets of newspaper to avoid damage on your journey home, and then, when you can hold it under a running tap, wash it gently to remove all traces of mud and sand. Put it in a well-aired place to dry, and then pick out the tracks with water colour or poster colour if you find the hard whiteness of the surface rather unattractive.

It is a good idea to record in a notebook every detail you can about the position of the earths, etc., the time of day and the movements of the animals. This will increase your enjoyment and enable you to find the exact spots again more easily in future.

Tracking your friends. Once you have trained your eyes to observe and interpret the subtler signs of the countryside, you may enjoy co-operating with your friends in a few trail-laying (and trail-finding) exercises. Your aim should be to set a course that can be followed with confidence, and yet is not blazed so obviously that any uninvolved person who happens upon them will notice the signs. Chalked arrows on walls and boulders, for instance, should *not* be used! Among the conventional signs you can use are these:

Arrows marked on the ground with small pebbles.
(Pointers in rough ground must not be too far apart or the trackers may miss them altogether.) Arrows may be scratched in the earth, or formed with twigs or small branches, but these methods may be a little more obvious.
A small stone touching a large stone: This can be used instead of an arrow to indicate a change of direction.

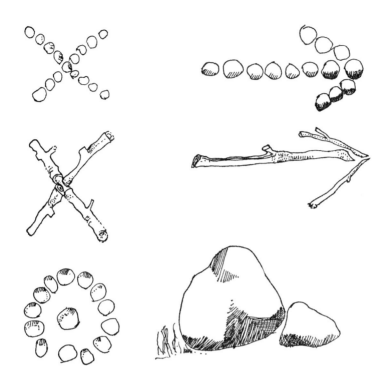

A small circle inside a large circle: This means 'I have gone Home'.
A cross like a multiplication sign: 'Not this way'.

Whatever signs you intend to use, you should get together with your
friends and agree upon your 'language' before you set out on a
tracking and trailing expedition. Then you will know exactly what to
look for, which is the secret of success.

Further reading
DAVID STEPHEN, *Watching Wild Life* (Collins).

Water colour painting

There are few outdoor hobbies that can give you more pleasure than drawing and painting. If you try picture-making when you are out for the day or away on holiday you will not only be recording the scenes that make you stop and stare, but you will be seeing more to enjoy in them. It can truly be said that sketching opens the eyes!

The materials most popular with outdoor artists include the graphic media, such as pencils and pens, and the painting media, such as oil colours and water colours. Of the latter, water colours are definitely the most convenient for travellers, for the amount of space they take up in one's luggage is negligible, and many subtle and charming effects can be obtained with them when they are handled by skilful craftsmen.

But water colours are definitely not the right medium to choose if you just want to slosh about happily, hoping that something rather good may emerge from your efforts. To produce worthwhile results with water colours you need a careful approach, great patience, and a knowledge of two or three quite difficult technical processes. As long as you understand that, there is no reason why you should not take water colours with you on your sketching expeditions, and why you should not thoroughly enjoy using them.

The essential qualities of water colours. To get the most out of water colours, you will have to appreciate their characteristic qualities, and the most important of these is—obvious as it may seem!— their wateriness. Unlike oil colours, with which an artist may build up a thick and opaque coating of pigment, water colours have to be used so thinly that they never lose their transparency or translucency. They depend for their luminosity on the lightness of the surface to which they are applied, and once this is hidden by too dense a film of pigment, the paint will lose all its vitality, bloom and beauty. You will have to bear this in mind from the moment you start choosing materials for a sketching jaunt. There will be no point in taking dark-toned paper with you, unless you are going to reinforce your work with opaque paints or 'body' colours. Then it will not be water colour painting at all but an entirely different technique.

Water colour paper. As well as being as fresh and as white as possible, the paper you choose for water colour painting must be thick enough and strong enough to stand up to quite a lot of washing and soaking. When you have had a considerable amount of practice you will probably be able to achieve the effects you want without any false starts or undue hesitancy, but until that happy day comes you will have to be prepared to do a certain amount of blotting and scrubbing out. That is the way you will learn the full resources of this rewarding medium.

Specially made papers that are suitable for use with water colours can be bought at all shops that stock artists' materials. Usually they are sold by the sheet, by the quire, or by the block or pad. Ordinary white drawing paper or cartridge paper may be used for small sketches, but all papers are better for being stretched first on a drawing board or a similar flat firm support if washes are to be laid over a large area of their surface.

To stretch a sheet of paper, soak it thoroughly in clean water. Hold it up and shake it slightly so that all surplus water drains and drips away. Then put it down on the flat surface on which you wish to stretch it and stick some lengths of gummed paper strip along the edges so that they overlap and hold it tightly down. When the paper dries it should be as taut as the parchment of a drum—a wonderful surface for painting on.

Brushes. A lot of the beauty of your water colour paintings will result from the way in which you apply the colours to the paper, so it is obvious that you should use only the very best brushes if you can possibly afford them.

Clearly, the brushes you choose will need to be soft and resilient rather than stiff and durable, since the colours with which they are to be charged will all be generously diluted with water. The very best brushes for water colour painting are known as 'Real Sables'. You will need one or two from the large grades (No. 9 or No. 10) for laying washes, one or two from the medium grades (No. 6 or No. 8) for general purposes, and one or two very fine brushes (No. 3 or No. 4) for the small details.

If you think that real sable brushes will be too expensive for you to use when you are just starting, you can buy cheaper substitutes that are usually known as 'squirrel' or 'ox-hair'. Whatever kind you use, you can keep your brushes in good condition almost indefinitely by remembering to wash every trace of paint carefully away from between the hairs before you put them away. Guide the hairs gently back into a point with the tips of your fingers as you put the brush down and you will find that the shape of the tip is preserved.

Colours. Most children are given at some time or another a box of assorted water colours. Usually these contain a number of solid colours in small china pans, but occasionally these are supplemented by a few semi-liquid colours, in collapsible tubes. You can use one of these compact and ready-assembled outfits if you like, but you may prefer to choose your own colours and to find some suitable box in which to carry them. China, plastic and japanned tin palettes can be purchased for mixing the colours in.

It is difficult to recommend any particular colours very positively, because all artists have their own ideas about the kind of colours likely to give the best results. Your stockist will have a wide range and this list may help you if you find the selection offered to you bewildering.

Yellow. Brilliant yellows that are at once pure in hue and reasonably permanent are hard to find. Cadmium yellow and aureolin (or cobalt yellow) are probably the best. A little duller are the safe but attractive earth colours, such as yellow ochre and raw sienna. These will provide a wide range of natural shades when mixed in varying strengths with the blue and green pigments mentioned later in this list.

Red. For all ordinary purposes, light red is entirely satisfactory. It is an earth colour, quite permanent, and will produce some beautiful greys when mixed with blue and yellow. If you want a more brilliant red in your colour box, try vermilion. If you want a subtle and lovely crimson, try rose-madder. Don't be tempted to try crimson lake or carmine. Attractive as these two colours are, neither is absolutely permanent.

Blue. Ideally, you should include two blues in your colour box. You will need a 'royal' blue, for use on its own, and for mixing with light red or rose-madder to make the dull violets and purples that are so useful for establishing the atmosphere of a landscape. You will also need a greenish blue, for mixing the rich shades of natural foliage. French ultramarine and cobalt blue are excellent alternatives for use as the 'warm' blue (which you choose, when you have tried both, will depend upon your personal taste). Cyanine blue or Leitch's blue is hard to beat for mixing greens. Prussian blue is powerful, and a lovely hue, but it cannot be absolutely relied on when made up as a water colour.

Green. Research chemists have given us the splendid and permanent viridian, or transparent oxide of chromium. The Old Masters were denied the use of this invaluable colour—they were born too early.

Black. Ivory black is one of the most useful colours you can include in your box, since you can produce an infinite number of subtle shades by mixing it with your stronger hues. Don't be tempted to apply it too thickly to your paper. It should never hide completely the brilliant white base that is to give all life and luminosity to your picture when it is finished.

Other colours you may be tempted to try when you want to increase your range are burnt sienna, which is a strong and useful earth brown, naples yellow, brown-madder and Indian red. Avoid using emerald green if you are the type of person who enjoys sucking a paint brush occasionally. It may not be absolutely permanent, but it is quite definitely poisonous.

Laying a wash. Before you set out to do any water colour painting out of doors you may like to practise laying a wash in the comparatively placid conditions of your home. The ability to lay an even film of pigment on your paper is a knack soon acquired. Mix in a saucer or paint pan a few spoonfuls of some rich colour such as Prussian blue, using only enough colour in the water to make a fluid like ink.

Tilt your painting surface until it is inclined at an angle of 30°-45°. It is almost impossible to apply water colours satisfactorily to paper lying flat on a level table top.

Then charge one of your largest brushes with colour and draw it across the upper edge of your paper so that it leaves behind a broad band of paint. As the paper is sloping, most of the excess moisture will flow to the lowest edge of this band and remain there.

Next, re-charge your brush and draw it again across the paper, keeping the second stroke parallel to the first, and allowing the upper edge of it to overlap by the smallest fraction of an inch the lower edge of the band left by the first stroke. The excess paint should then flow downwards over the newly painted surface, collecting once more at the 'dry' lower edge.

Continue in this way, working down the paper as carefully and deliberately as you can, taking care not to drag your brush twice over any part of the paper. As you near the bottom of the space to be filled, dilute the paint you are using with increasing amounts of clean water until it is practically colourless. In this way you will be able to produce the same effect of graduation as you will find in a cloudless sky, which is almost invariably stronger in tone and colour at the zenith than it is near the horizon.

Examine carefully the surface you have painted when it has had a chance to dry and you will find that it has a lovely smooth fresh quality, not unlike that of the shell of a newly laid hen's egg. You will be able to achieve this serene quality in your work when you are actually out sketching if you do not labour too long over any surface.

Starting a sketch. Once you have collected your equipment and tried out your brushes and paints you will probably be eager to start some work out of doors. You will be able to manage without an easel by holding your painting surface on your knees, but you will find a folding stool a most useful piece of equipment.

When you are looking for somewhere to sit or stand it is not necessary to find a thatched cottage, a windmill, a rustic bridge, or any other ready-made 'picturesque' subject. Often, a stretch of agricultural land, a tree-shaded reach of a river, or some pleasantly proportioned buildings will provide the ingredients for a satisfying pictorial composition, as long as there is one single feature that can be given some slight emphasis to make it act as the 'centre of interest'.

A composition that is made up of a number of features which are all of equal importance may have a certain monotony.

Once you have found a subject that appeals to you, you will have to decide how much of the landscape before you is going to be included in your picture. You can use a viewfinder to help you to make this decision, or you can make a rough sketch, on a spare piece of paper, which need not contain any details at all. Then you can make a preliminary drawing on the paper on which you intend to paint, using, preferably, a sharp pencil. The amount of detail you include in this study may vary according to the circumstances in which you are working. Some artists, intent on making quick, spontaneous records of fleeting effects of light will make rapid notes in direct brushwork without using a pencil at all. Others, who are tackling intricate architectural subjects, will make precise studies in pencil before they mix any colours at all.

The 'composition' or structure of a water colour painting is as important as that of an oil painting, and you will have to be prepared to make some slight alterations in your representation of the scene in front of you if the design of your picture is to be completely satisfying. It is rarely advisable to have the centre of interest exactly in the middle of a picture, for instance, for then the composition may be cut unpleasingly into two competing halves. It may be necessary to reduce the height of a clump of trees so that its shape balances that of a smaller clump. It may help the composition if you move the posts of a roadside fence to new positions a little further away from the edge of the highway. You will soon learn how to adjust your preliminary drawing so that the eye is led pleasantly and easily on a 'conducted tour' of the picture.

If a large proportion of your picture is to be taken up with sky, it is usually safest to lay this in first, as it will normally be the lightest part of the composition. Many artists like to paint the more distant

features in next, before the washes used for painting the sky near the horizon are quite dry. This ensures a certain softness in the edges, and gives a delightfully natural mistiness to the deep recesses of a picture.

Whatever part of your picture you are painting, don't be afraid to simplify. If you look closely at (say) a hillside in the middle of a landscape, you may be able to see woods and hedges and buildings on it, but it may be much more effective as an ingredient of a picture if it is represented by a flat shape or silhouette, without any texture or detail. Study some of the most successful paintings by eminent water colourists such as Turner, Cotman and Philip Wilson Steer and you will see how a few patches of flat, unworked colour can be combined most convincingly to suggest a romantic and overgrown landscape.

The foreground of a water colour painting is often the most difficult part of the picture to complete satisfactorily. Large solid objects such as boats and tree trunks tend to look heavy and un-attractive when they are allowed to take up more room than their shapes justify. Many difficulties can be avoided if the last stages of picture-making are foreseen when a composition is first planned. You may be able to leave out some particularly awkward feature, for instance, just by shifting your viewpoint. There is no point in spoil-ing an attractive painting by including any prominent masses which would look bold and dramatic if tackled in oil colours, but which may be beyond the resources of the slighter medium.

Mounting your work. No water colour sketch can ever be seen to its best possible advantage unless it has a wide band of some white

189

or neutral material all round it, to separate it from the distracting colours and shapes of its immediate surroundings. That is why it is important to mount your outdoor work as soon as you can after you get it home, even if you are not going to glaze and frame it.

As a temporary measure, you can stick each sketch lightly on to a large sheet of white, buff or pale grey paper, so that you can decide at your leisure on the proportions and colour of the permanent mount.

If you use card or mounting board for the permanent surround you can fix the picture directly to the front surface with small spots of glue or paste, or with the attachment strips used for mounting photographs, or you can use a very sharp knife or steel-backed razor blade to make a chamfer at 45° round a pleasantly spaced cut-out area. Use a steel rule or straight edge to guide your blade if you try chamfer-cutting. If you 'make do' with a wooden ruler you will probably slice some slivers off the leading edge!

Further reading
ADRIAN HILL, *The Beginners' Book of Water Colour Painting* (Blandford Press).
ROWLAND HILDER, *Starting with Watercolour* (Studio Vista).

Whittling

Most boys enjoy whittling, and are ready to carve any suitable piece of wood they find so that it resembles a human head, an animal, or even, if they are exceptionally dexterous, a flexible chain with interlocking links. It is a pleasant pastime, but like all hobbies that involve the use of sharp knives it calls for a certain amount of care if accidents are to be avoided.

Choosing woods. Most hard woods are very attractive when they are carved and polished, but you should not choose them for your earliest attempts at whittling. If you find a piece of applewood or cherry when you are out for a walk in the country, take it home, by all means, but leave it to 'season' in a dry, well-ventilated place until you have had a chance to practise on some more tractable timbers, such as white or yellow pine, or willow.

A knife for whittling. Most penknives can be used for whittling, but no blade, even one of the finest steel, will give good results unless it is kept really sharp. An oilstone, or access to one, is therefore almost indispensable, and the knife edge should be touched up on it at frequent intervals.

Holding your work. You can hold in a vice the wood you are going to whittle, or you can hold it in your hand. If you decide on the latter course, you will be helped by the fact that you can turn your work easily as it begins to take shape, but you will have to be careful to keep the knife moving away from you, in case it slips.

Most skilled whittlers hold their knives in such a way that accidents are fairly easily avoided. To use this grip (if you are right-handed) hold the wood in your left hand and the knife in your right hand. Then put the end of your left hand thumb on your right hand thumbnail and you will find it quite easy to make both hands co-operate in cutting, braking, and guiding the knife blade.

Should any occasion arise when it is absolutely essential that you should cut towards yourself, you can minimize the danger by letting the finger tips of your left hand rest on the fingers of your right hand to provide the driving power for the cut. If, then, you let your right hand thumb rest on the wood, it will help to steady your hand, and it will also be ready to act as an extra brake when one is needed. See that your wood is held very firmly or all these precautions will be in vain!